Supervision
in
teacher education

Supervision
in
teacher education

A COUNSELLING AND PEDAGOGICAL APPROACH

· · · · · · · · · ·

EDGAR STONES

METHUEN & CO. LTD: LONDON

9515

First published in 1984 by
Methuen & Co. Ltd
11 New Fetter Lane, London
EC4P 4EE
© 1984 Edgar Stones
Printed in Great Britain at the
University Press, Cambridge

British Library
Cataloguing in Publication Data

Stones, Edgar
Supervision in teacher education.
1. Teachers—In-service
training—Great Britain
I. Title
370'.7'330941   LB2157.G7

ISBN 0–416–34980–3
ISBN 0–416–34990–0 Pbk

Contents

Introduction

Supervise: (1) To direct or oversee; (2) To watch over so as to maintain order
Counsel: to give advice or guidance to

Seated one day at the typewriter making notes on supervision, when the machine hiccupped and produced *super-vision*. In a blinding flash I knew what it was all about. The qualification for becoming a supervisor was super-vision. Further thought produced an analysis of *super-vision*. What were its constituent skills? Naturally enough they all seemed to be connected with sight. In the first place a person with *super-vision* would need to have acute *eyesight* to see what was happening in the classroom. Second, a person would need *insight* to understand the significance of what was happening, *foresight* to see what could be happening, *hindsight* to see what should have happened and didn't, and *second sight* to know how to get what should have happened and didn't to happen next time. As may be inferred, I consider supervision a fairly complex activity.

Most training institutions are not troubled with my hang-ups. It seems that they believe that super-vision is inherited or, at any rate, innate. By and large it is detected on interview when candidates are quizzed on a variety of subjects usually related to the disciplines they will be asked to lecture in.

The first task I ever had as a neophyte supervisor of student teachers was to arrange transport to get them to their practice schools. A friendly colleague inducted me into the mysteries of timetabling and shrewd dealing with coach companies so that with application I eventually became reasonably competent at getting the students to the right place at the right time. When I failed to do so, the fact was made clear by both students and colleagues. On the other hand, nobody ever thought it necessary to advise me about the supervision of the students under my charge. I suppose this was because I had come to the college from school teaching and therefore should know about these things. In retrospect, if the college had taken the same line of reasoning about my other activities, I could have been spared the induction into the transport arranger part of my role because I had had experience of travelling on buses.

There may be another reason for this experience. My colleagues may have felt diffident about attempting to induct someone into a role that was ill defined and very little understood. Although this was never made explicit, I suspect that it was an important factor. That experience was many years ago but things have changed uncomfortably little since then, and the supervision of student teachers is still a very much neglected subject despite its centrality to the whole process of teacher education.

The preoccupation with administrative detail that I experienced is just one aspect of the messiness of the conception of the role of supervisor. I discuss others later. However, in the discussion that follows, I take the implicit dilemma posed in the two definitions at the beginning and suggest means whereby it might be resolved. In the process the appropriateness of the first definition is questioned and the implications of the latter analysed and appraised. Commonly held conceptions of the role of a supervisor as someone whose sole function is to go into schools to observe student teachers and make suggestions about their teaching are fundamentally questioned.

The appraisal suggests that the role of supervisor is more complex than is normally acknowledged, but also that it can, and should, be seen as a much higher level activity than it is currently. Possibilities for the development of the role towards the production of more effective teachers are discussed, with the main emphasis being placed on forms of supervision that relate practical teaching and its appraisal to theoretical studies.

The complexity of the role as proposed may appear formidable, but I believe that that is the way supervision is, even though it is not currently so acknowledged. It may be that the task of supervision needs reconceptualizing as a co-operative operation rather than a lone ranger exercise. The book discusses these kinds of possibilities and suggests ways that may help realize them, drawing on a decade's experience of supervisor training in which new approaches were developed. That experience taught me the inappropriateness of the current nomenclature, hence the sub-title of the book. I hope readers will find the emphasis justified and come to share my prejudices.

A note on 'training'

I have used the expression 'teacher training' throughout the book. I should like to emphasize, however, that this usage is entirely for convenience in referring to those aspects of teacher education that are particularly concerned with the students' preparation for teaching. There is no implication of low level routine or drill type activity; in fact the precise opposite is the case. The study of the practice and theory of pedagogy is held to be as exacting and highly educative an activity as any other aspect of a course of teacher education.

1

· · · · · · · · · ·

The way we are now

The supervision of student teachers is a much understudied subject in Britain. This may be because teaching itself has, until recent years, received little attention from researchers in education. Preoccupations such as the study of individual and group differences may well have deflected attention from the study of how to help people to learn (Stones 1978a). The recent upsurge of interest in classroom studies, however, is not showing much evidence of being influenced by, or making a contribution to, theories relating to human learning or teaching. Given this context it is perhaps not surprising that many teacher educators still implement methods of supervision that have been characterized as atheoretical, idiosyncratic, poorly conceptualized, of doubtful efficacy and in some cases probably harmful (MacAleese 1976, Greenfield 1977, Stones and Morris 1972b).

Strong words, perhaps, and ones that many teacher educators would probably wish to contest. But there is no denying that in many institutions concerned with teacher preparation there is no awareness that problems exist in the field of supervision. This lack of awareness is manifest in the fact that supervisors of practical teaching in Britain, for example (but also in the USA, Brodbelt 1980), are frequently recruited from staff who have not made a study of any of the foundation disciplines of education, apart from a limited exposure during their own teacher training, and even those that have studied further in the field of education are extremely unlikely to have given thought to the theory and practice of supervision. It is also unlikely that they will be inducted into methods of supervision, and criteria for assessment of practical teaching are likely to be unexplicated (Stones and Morris 1972a). The implicit assumptions that inform such practices seem to be that supervision is a methodological and curriculum matter that merits no pedagogical attention. In my view this is a complete misconception that ignores the complexity of human learning and underestimates the difficulties of helping others to learn, that is, teaching. Above all, current practice grotesquely misconceives the nature of supervision, reducing it to little more than the ritual attention to the cosmetics of teaching, whereas its ostensible *raison d'être* bespeaks one of the most complex of human interactions: teaching teachers to teach. If teaching is complex, the meeting between supervisor and student teacher should be the quintessential teaching-learning encounter.

In fact supervision in many teacher education institutions is seen as relatively unproblematic. Prevalent policies of staff recruitment and training rarely concern themselves with the question. Staff are recruited in general on the strength of their subject knowledge or expertise in the field of educational studies *which need not and probably does not include familiarity with pedagogy*. Once appointed, neophyte lecturers rapidly discover that they are expected to exercise powers they did not suspect they possessed. In many colleges, supervision is an occupational hazard of all staff whether they were hired to teach maths, movement or method. Initiation rites are rare and in places where teaching practice takes place in the first week or two of the course, a new recruit could be supervising students within a few days of taking up a post. Any induction the beginning supervisor may experience is likely to be concerned with administration and organization or such things as the place of practical teaching in the course structure. There will, in the main, be little discussion of the actual process of guiding beginning teachers in their classroom activities, or of the aims of those activities; and rarely will there be any explication of the possible links between the students' practical teaching and the work they do in their theoretical studies. The overriding assumption in most institutions that underlies this approach to the induction of student teachers into practical teaching is still the one Morris and I drew attention to in 1972, namely that teaching is best learned by observing practitioners, which we referred to as *Sitting with Nellie.*

With such a perspective it is not unreasonable that super-visors concern themselves more with timetables and transport to schools than with the systematic consideration of pedago-gical theory that might inform the students' own teaching. Nor is it denigratory of individual tutors to suggest that people hired as subject specialists, or education tutors hired because of their profound knowledge of the academic study of specific aspects of educational theory, might lack the expertise to make the practice-theory connections. The problem is a collective one. Pedagogy has been given little or no attention by training institutions anywhere and institutions have signalled their low opinion of the subject by assuming that since, by and large, the staff they recruit are experienced teachers, supervisors will be able to augment the guidance provided by the teacher in the practice schools and thereby induct students into the art of teaching. The view taken in this book is that the appren-ticeship view of teacher training not only constitutes a profound restraint on the development of a useful pedagogy capable of transforming teaching, but that it also devalues the role of the supervisor, thus creating an additional impediment to the production of teachers with a grasp of generalizable principles related to their practice.

The nature of the problem

Perhaps the biggest problem has been the one mentioned earlier: the fact that teacher trainers and their institutions do not perceive there to be a problem and in fact little is done in the way of formal induction into the role of the supervisor as pedagogical adviser in British training institutions. The im-plication seems to be that the unproblematic nature of teaching is such that it is easily grasped by a few years' exposure in the classroom and that the process is much the same wherever it is observed. Some researchers in the field in recent years have encouraged this belief. Indeed, many studies seem to assume that there is a standard pedagogy homogeneous across schools, and focus on such things as 'formal' versus 'informal' teaching, expository or discovery teaching or internal classroom organization. Even in studies of classroom interaction using analytical schedules which record in great detail what happens in teaching, the categories tend to be descriptive of teacher and pupil activities *as they are at present* without any relation *to how they might be* to facilitate learning.

If there is a common pedagogy across schools the apparent complacency of training staff about current modes of supervision may be both cause and consequence of the current state of that pedagogy. If pedagogy itself is seen as unproblematic, then it follows that supervision will also be so perceived. And if supervisors take this view and act accordingly the cycle is complete. It does seem that this is the case. In many spheres, and particularly in secondary and higher education, the staple mode of teaching still seems to be the transmission mode, where teaching is viewed as telling. With a view like this it is reasonable for supervisors to concentrate on such things as voice production and associated elocutory activities, together with ways to enhance the effects of telling such as chalkboard presentation and the teacher's position in the classroom. Where teaching is equated with telling the important thing is seen as what is being told. Hence the attraction of the argument that the important thing in teacher training is the subject specialism.

There is little doubt that this simplistic view is one of the most intractable obstacles to the development of effective teaching. Its persistence in teacher education is serious since it endorses in practice the 'transmission' view of teaching. It thus implicitly denies the existence of a body of theory and practice in teaching susceptible to serious study and implementation. Thus the focus of most supervisory advice to student teachers is on the cosmetic activities referred to above. The end result should give serious cause for concern as recent HMI reports testify (Arnold 1981, DES 1981). They report lack of transferability of pupil learning to new situations and inability to solve problems related to the learning. Given the predominant teaching mode this is not surprising: all too often what is transmitted is shadow not substance.

Words and meanings

Transmission teaching in institutes for teacher preparation reflects a fundamental irony common to all educational institutions where it is to be found. It is that while language is the most powerful tool in human learning, it can also be an obstacle. Words are easily dispensed in lectures, seminars or other media. The trouble is that the medium (words) is taken to be the message, whereas words are only the carriers (symbols) of the message (the meanings or concepts). Teachers teaching words without the underlying concepts are teaching at one of the simplest levels of learning, stimulus-response learning.

The special irony inherent in the employment of this kind of approach in teacher preparation is particularly clear in the field of pedagogy. Staff inducting student teachers into the principles and practice of teaching by depending in the main on verbal transmission declare by their actions either lack of faith in their expositions on the subject of human learning, or ignorance of a pedagogy that can help to enhance those kinds of learning that are typically human. Such a pedagogy would preclude current transmission approaches to teaching and teacher training since it involves more complex and time consuming activities than merely talking and listening or taking notes. Thus obsessive 'syllabus covering', traversing vast tracks of verbalizing on, for example, the nature of human learning and its systematic enhancement by teachers, would be replaced by activities in which teachers would be involved *of necessity* in the examination of principles and their application to problematic situations involving students' learning.

The paradoxical thing about most present teacher training courses is that if the staff or the institutions took cognizance of some of the most well known of principles from learning theories, they would realize that learning a concept (in our case the concept of good teaching) from a random set of exemplars such as is provided by observing other teachers is, to say the least, problematic. And a key aspect of the learning of concepts is that it is not possible to learn a concept from a series of non-exemplars of that concept. In common sense terms, if student teachers see only poor teachers in their apprenticeship they are unlikely to arrive at the notion of what good teaching is. In practice it is unlikely that many teachers will exhibit only non-criterial attributes of good teaching, but unless the students have some idea of what the criterial attributes are they will be completely unable to evaluate the teaching they observe. And unless their tutors in turn make an attempt to present positive and negative exemplars in some systematic way, they are leaving the students to induce the critical attributes of good teaching from a randomly experienced sequence of events about which they are rarely given confirmatory or disconfirmatory feedback.

Supervision: active or passive?

This incoherent conceptualization of teaching is a central difficulty inherent in the apprenticeship approach to teacher training. It arises from the practice referred to earlier of focusing on *teachers* rather than *teaching* and expecting student teachers to learn to teach by watching other teachers at work. In this approach the supervisor is predominantly passive and in only infrequent contact with the students and that contact is likely to be seen by the student as adjudicatory rather than helpful, a point I return to later.

But there are many other problems. The teachers student teachers are expected to imitate, that is, the *master teachers,* even if they are highly experienced and skilled, can offer a student only a limited set of skills, attitudes and personality traits. And the selection of skills and techniques will reflect the master teacher's values, experiences and personality. The student's values, experiences and personality will be at least marginally, and at most radically different from those of the master teacher. In its extreme form this encourages the student to copy isolated bits of teaching behaviour, of attitudes and of relationships as being effective. But the effectiveness of these bits of behaviour may well hinge on their being part of a total pattern of behaviour: when fragmented and adopted by another they may be ineffective or even harmful. Further, this approach is only superficially easy to follow. Learning by imitation has limited effectiveness; learning a skill as complex as teaching by imitation is likely to be particularly unproductive.

A further disadvantage of this approach is that it does not allow the student to go beyond the teaching observed. This teaching may be excellent but it cannot be exhaustively excellent; there will certainly be areas of teaching excellence that are not illustrated by any one master teacher and more appropriate ways of doing things than those the master teacher employs.

There is one other very difficult problem connected with this approach to teacher training: there is little consensus about what a master teacher is. That is, there are no universally accepted criteria to help us to identify master teachers. Thus the current most popular approaches to teacher training have serious disadvantages. Based as they are on an apprenticeship model that stresses imitation without any clear indication of the qualities to emulate, they are fundamentally unhelpful to beginning teachers and at the same time conservative so that it is difficult to break the circle to introduce new procedures that might be more beneficial to student teachers.

Assessment of teaching

The problems of reaching consensus on what constitutes a master teacher are reflected in the assessment of student teaching practice. The literature on teacher effectiveness would probably fill a fair-sized library and yet there is just no general agreement on what the criteria should be. There is, however, no shortage of confident assertions by staff of teacher training institutions that they 'know one when they see one', the 'one' referring either to a 'good' or a 'bad' teacher. The problem is that the perceptions of these assessors are various: one person's good is another person's bad or indifferent, and this is the case even if, at the end of the day, when the final assessment chips are down, agreement is reached among examiners. Consensus is arrived at for all sorts of complex reasons that do not necessarily include agreement over criteria of teacher effectiveness and which may not be unconnected with the institutions' widespread non-explication of their criteria for student teacher assessment (Stones and Morris 1972a).

In recent years many training institutions have attempted to remedy this situation and to introduce a degree of rigour and objectivity into the assessment of practice teaching by producing schedules for assessment. These schedules itemize those aspects of teaching performance thought to be criterial in satisfactory teaching. Student teachers are awarded marks on a scale for each aspect by supervisors or co-operating teachers. Examples of items from schedules are: 'clarity of aims, pacing of the lesson, skill in explaining and narrating, quality of voice and speech habits, presentation advanced with appropriate pace and time, voice clear attractive and well modulated, blackboard well used, lesson method suitable'. It will not have escaped notice that most of the items relate to transmission methods of teaching. But readers might well be interested in the fact that the items were taken from British, American and Australian schedules currently in use, and the last comes from a teacher assessment form used in Britain in the nineteenth century. *Plus ça change!*

Whether schedules or global methods of assessment are used does not affect one of the central difficulties of current supervisory practice. I refer to the question of the supervisor's role as adjudicator of teaching competence and arbiter of a student's right to enter the teaching profession. No matter how supportive the supervisor, the day of judgement eventually arrives when a grade has to be awarded. Not unnaturally many students take out insurance by attempting to fathom out what in their classroom activity is likely to be rewarded and then doing their best to provide it without any reference to its pedagogical worth. This student ploy is often referred to as 'impression management', an apt appellation for a very pervasive phenomenon (see Shipman 1967). Sorenson (Stones 1975b) had some interesting answers from students when he investigated their perceptions about what was likely to get them good grades. 'Do as you are told. Toady up to the supervisor. Prepare lessons in advance. Keep absolute control all the time' were some of the criteria they advanced. Not items commonly found in schedules of assessment!

Supervision present and future

Currently in training institutions generally, many staff who undertake supervision, being subject teachers, are not engaged in any way in introducing their students to the education disciplines that might possibly have something to say of value to teaching. That task is the province of the staff of the education department. Thus the neglect of a pedagogy that unites theoretical principles and practical teaching is doubly reinforced by the assumption that any subject teacher can supervise practical teaching competently, and by the practice of education tutors who lecture about the disciplines of education but not of teaching. Could it be the neglect of theoretical studies directly related to teaching that leads to the commonly observed assertion by student teachers that teaching practice is the most useful part of the course? The acute form of Hobson's choice syndrome? Whether this is so or not, I have little doubt that when students are offered rational theoretical principles that are demonstrably useful in practical teaching, they are more than ready to examine and, if convinced, to embrace them and take a new view of the relationship between theoretical studies and practical teaching.

The question of the nature of the relationship between supervisor, student and co-operating teacher is the other central aspect of current and possible future approaches to supervision. If the relationship depicted above is held to be appropriate, then there is little more to say. If, however, it is not, and if training institutions and supervisory staff have a genuine desire to improve relationships and the efficacy of the supervision afforded, then it is imperative that they consider how their current procedures can be modified to bring about this amelioration. To illustrate the way some teachers perceive the relationship between teacher and supervisor as it is now and as it might be I turn to another investigation, this time a provocative/evocative study by Blumberg (1976).

Blumberg devised a projective test in an attempt to establish teachers' perceptions of supervisors as they are now and supervisors as they would like them to be. His approach was to ask teachers to write descriptions of the houses they imagined supervisors as they are now might live in, and descriptions of houses they imagined supervisors in the future might live in. Four groups of four teachers wrote descriptions. The descriptions merit attention. They run as follows:

TWO DESCRIPTIONS OF IMAGINED HOUSES
OF SUPERVISORS AS THEY ARE NOW

(1) One approaches the house via a long winding driveway. You cannot see the house from the road. The lawn surrounding

the house is very green because it is made of astroturf. The house itself is square and has a flat roof. There is nothing romantic about it. There are no windows in the house. A number of things strike you as you enter. Everything is in its place. The furniture is very austere and it is nailed to the floor. There is a picture on the wall that is a flow chart in colour of administrative positions. Diplomas hang next to the flow chart. There are floral arrangements composed of artificial flowers. The lighting system is stark and very bright. The house is very clean. It has a central cleaning system with vacuums in the walls. In the house are janitorial supplies and text books. There are also disconnected bodies sitting in straight rows.

(2) The house is located in the suburbs on a large plot. It is very distant from the road thus seeming to convey a need for privacy. Inside the house there is a 'receiving place' for people who enter. There also seems to be a 'safe place' that the occupant uses for retreating. There are lots of mail boxes and mail chutes. Piles of mail are constantly forming in big bins which must be filled by 3 p.m. The library has floor to ceiling book cases. But the books are not accessible because the bottom shelves are empty. The books are not sorted. There is a medicine cabinet that is filled with Band-Aids, assorted remedies and lots of Kleenex. There is also a telescope in the house but it is very narrow enabling the viewer to see only a little bit of the house and also a coffee urn, but the urn is in a different room. In the conference room there are pictures of the supervisor's family and his/her diplomas. There is a picture of the graduation when the diplomas were awarded. These pictures are well lighted. There are also framed testimonials and autographed pictures of previous clients. Curiously the clients of the supervisor don't have ears so there is a megaphone at the supervisor's place at the conference table.

TWO DESCRIPTIONS OF IMAGINARY HOUSES OF SUPERVISORS OF THE FUTURE

(1) The house is a round one. There are lots of two-way windows. It is located in a sort of park-like atmosphere. The house seems friendly and can be expanded. It is all on one floor and has a large revolving entrance door making it easy to enter

or to leave. The fact that it is round and on one floor conveys an egalitarian not bureaucratic atmosphere where all resources have equal input. In the inside, around the wall, there are lots of partitioned enclosures each with a revolving door. The partitions separate the enclosures from a 'commons' area but do not totally enclose them. The 'commons' is used for discussions between the occupant of the house and visitors.

(2) The house is in the country with two acres of land around it. It is an older house and is painted white with green trim. The doors are never locked. On the outside there is a 'fun' garden where people can gather for a party. The house is furnished very comfortably. There is a fireplace and furniture you can sink into. There are many guest rooms and a large kitchen with a big table. The walls in the kitchen are made of brick and are decorated with many pots and pans. The coffee pot is always on. The stairwell leading to the guest rooms is very large. There are French doors that open to the garden. The house conveys a style of Old America.

As Blumberg says, you do not have to be a skilled psychodiagnostician to make sense of these imaginary houses. Nor, I would add, need you subscribe to any sort of depth psychological theory to see that the teachers are saying something significant. Blumberg plucks out of the descriptions certain key concepts that seem to characterize the image of supervisors. At present they are distant, the climate is artificial, unimaginative, closed to new ideas. Neatness, order and rigidity are noted. Formality and defensiveness, the need for status and an atmosphere of busy work are apparent. (Organizing school visits?) In the future the teachers saw openness and accessibility, friendliness and lack of bureaucracy. The supervisor is seen more as a consultant and his house exudes warmth and has a relaxed though businesslike atmosphere.

Supervision today, in this investigation, as in the one discussed earlier, seems to be characterized by strain and tension. Supervisors are seen as distant and much of what goes on in supervision is artificial and ritualized. Of course there is no claim that supervision is all of a piece wherever it is to be found. There is no doubt that many supervisors are extremely supportive and resemble the ones depicted in the fantasies of the future. Indeed, the recent report by British Inspectors of Schools (DES 1982) makes reference to this and quotes one student as saying that his tutor's visits were unintimidating, honest, constructive and generally appreciated. Thus the studies reported are illustrative, not advanced as evidence. However, there is a very real difficulty in that the problem discussed relating to supervision are problems of the role itself and its institutional setting, so that personality differences among supervisors while clearly important in the process, can only be one part of it. As it is more effective for student teachers to focus on *teaching* than *teachers*, it is more helpful for us to focus on *supervision* than *supervisors*.

Evidence discussed elsewhere suggests that the studies reported above are not unique in the nature of their findings, even if they differ in degree. Blumberg makes one further important point. The problems of supervision discussed in this chapter are not the product of evil or ignorant people so much as of educational structures and attitudes. To effect ameliorative change will necessitate the reappraisal of both, and of the procedures of supervision as they are currently found. I consider some possible approaches to these problems in the pages which follow.

2

Supervision reviewed

Seekers after truth in the lexical labyrinth of literature relating to supervision will not get lost if they stick to the British paths. Nor will they find much in the way of truth. As I suggested at the outset, the subject has not been noted for the attention devoted to it by indigenous researchers, so that exploration of those few avenues is likely to be unfruitful if expeditious. Venturers along the American trails, on the other hand, will need a large ball of thread and a lot of time when they enter the maze, but the rewards of exploration could be substantial. However they could also be misleading, and instead of finding treasure the enquirers could well find themselves strangers in a strange land, uncertain about the significance of what they are beholding.

From which excursion the reader may have surmised that although the American scene, as far as the study of supervision is concerned, is more expansive than the British, its topography is unfamiliar. The word is the same; the concept is different. By and large the connotations of *supervision* in Britain and her erstwhile colonies relate to activities of staff of training institutions in relation to students on initial teacher training. In the USA the connotations embrace the activities of a parapedagogical corps of people in a superordinate relationship with practising teachers in schools, as well as those activities cognate to British conceptions. Thus the teachers who built Blumberg's houses were real teachers and not student teachers in initial training, and the supervisors they had in mind were people who resembled heavier versions of British local inspectors or advisers. Heavier because of their continuous monitoring of teachers coupled with their power of recommending termination of teachers' contracts; a power that contrasts with the once and for all monitoring at the end of probation in British schools. It is as well to be aware of this important difference when surveying the literature, especially since accountability became so salient a factor on the American scene. There is no implication, however, that the American literature deals exclusively with the supervision of practising teachers, and in fact a substantial amount of work reporting on aspects of the supervision of students on initial training is available, although British readers need to make some cultural adjustment when contemplating it. A good first text might well be the *Handbook of Educational Supervision* (Marks *et al.* 1979). Its 699 pages might well cause culture shock to British readers. A quick glance will reveal an almost alien world at the same time as it illustrates the nature of the job and the considerable administrative load involved in it.

In the pages which follow I focus specifically on the literature on supervision that deals with initial teacher training. Thus questions concerning the supervision of inservice teachers will be discussed only to the extent that they are common to both inservice and preservice teacher training. Just what is the extent of overlap between the procedures in the two cases depends on how one conceives the key aspects of supervision. As I suggested earlier, concerns of an administrative nature loom large in much of the British supervisor's activities, and this aspect of supervision may well have much in common with the concerns of American inservice supervision. Significantly the lines of demarcation between classificatory categories in the literature wander fuzzily between teacher education and administration. The types of administrative activity, however, differ in the two countries so that it is likely that little benefit will be gained from comparative study. More important, however, I believe, is the fact that the administrative problems are peripheral not central to the key aims of supervision and are more likely than not to be institutional-specific; therefore pedagogy, not administration, is the theme of this book.

Given the greater stress on accountability in the USA, one might reasonably expect problems of assessment to loom larger in American than in British practice and research.

Ironically, however, the bulk of the work on supervision in Britain, such as it is, is concerned with assessment, even though the quality control activities of school supervisors in the American sense are not a problem. But perhaps this is not surprising in view of the predilection of the hegemonists in British education to be much more interested in the grading of students than in their growth. Having said that, to judge from the extent of the literature on the subject in countries where there is a system of teacher education, problems of the assessment of practical teaching are of central importance at all levels and in all institutions, everywhere, and I do not think it too wild a guess to suggest that it is the aspect of supervision that has attracted more attention than any other in recent times. It is, therefore, a subject that no consideration of supervision can ignore and I now turn to some of its salient aspects as they emerge from the literature.

The assessment of teaching

HOW LONG IS A PIECE OF STRING?

This was the question that came to mind when I was asked to talk to a group of teacher educators about the assessment of practical teaching. The organizers of the seminar must have liked it because they adopted it for the title of the monograph that eventually emerged (Stones 1975b). This was some years ago but I have little reason to change my views or my title. In my experience, however, there are many people in teacher education in Britain who are convinced they know exactly how long a piece of string is and who raise their eyebrows when one expresses diffidence in advancing a view. The trouble is their estimates frequently do not agree, a fact that rarely emerges in any definitive way except in work on the trainers of raters of teaching.

When examples of teaching are rated independently by different people, it frequently occurs that there is little agreement among them. Wragg (1982), Saunders and Saunders (1980) and Morrison and McIntyre (1969) report on recent research in this field including some which compared different approaches to assessment. In order to cope with this problem of lack of rater agreement it is customary, before conducting any research into the use of classroom observation instruments, to train the observers and involve them in discussions of the methods in order to enhance agreement.

In normal day-to-day assessment supervisors and examiners will compare notes and indulge in academic oriental bargaining until all differences are split and consciences cleared by the diffusing glow of satisfaction in having done a difficult job expertly, honestly and equitably. In fact consensus is reached essentially by fudging the question of the criteria of competent teaching; pooled prejudices produce spurious agreement.

Whether agreement is, in fact, reached is neither here nor there unless the ratings are demonstrably valid. Since the criteria of competence are not explicated except at the most global level, 'he/she is a good teacher', the question of validity is not addressed (Stones 1975b, Hogan 1983). If, as I suggest, pupils' cognitive, affective and psychomotor learning is taken to be *the* criterion, the problematic nature of teaching assessment becomes even more pronounced in view of the enormous difficulty in arriving at generally agreed measures of such learning.

My disquiet about the smugness of most current approaches to assessment was given substance by an investigation Sidney Morris and I conducted in which we obtained information about methods of assessment of teaching in practically all training institutions in England, Wales and Northern Ireland (Stones and Morris 1972a). I do not wish to go into detail about the findings here, but the information we obtained led to two vital conclusions which were that training institutions were rewarding quite different things when they assessed students and that there was no real identifiable consensual criterion of teaching competence. Just as alarming was the fact that few institutions actually mentioned pupil learning as an element in the assessment of teaching.

Around the same time Hore (1971) had found that 'attractive' women students got better grades on student teaching when assessed by men. Earlier Wiseman and Start (1965) had found that teachers whose personality was similar to the rater obtained higher grades than those whose personality was different. These are just two among many reports illustrating the use of what might, justly in my view, be regarded as irrelevant influences in arriving at an assessment of teaching ability. More recently, McCulloch (1979) conducted an investigation similar to the Stones and Morris (1972a) research. She found a situation that had changed little over the intervening years. Idiosyncratic criteria, disagreement as to what is being assessed and unexplicated criteria of assessment all point to an unchanged obscurity in this aspect of teacher education held to be so important by so many senior people in the field. In view of the persistence of this state of affairs I am immensely puzzled by the fact that when I suggest that perhaps we ought to give up the practice of assessing and awarding teaching practice marks, strong persons in meetings of influential educational bodies fall about in hilarious incredulity. My puzzlement is not alleviated by the fact that very, very few people who have completed a course actually fail teaching practice and practically all that 'fail' recoup their 'failure' within the year by 'retaking' their teaching practice assessment.

I wish to stress that this low failure rate does not necessarily imply 'low standards'. To a great extent it is accounted for by in-course advice and counselling leading to student withdrawal from the teaching profession. But the important point is that those who do go on to take the final practical teaching assessment almost all pass. Stones and Webster (1983), in a survey of institutions in England and Wales, found that, of all students completing a course of teacher education, failure rates over the previous five years were 1.5 per cent or less for PGCE courses and 0.8 per cent or less for B.Ed. courses. Of those completing the course and retaking the practical teaching assessment, less than 0.4 per cent of PGCE students and less than 0.16 per cent of B.Ed. students actually failed. In view of student withdrawals and the very small percentage actually failing the course, my suggestion is that it is a great waste of time, effort and resources to persist in the rituals of final teaching assessment, unless, of course, they serve, as they may well do, a function other than that of student assessment. Cogan (1976) draws attention to a similar situation in the assessment of in-service teachers. The less naive might suggest that perhaps the hilarity I mentioned above is less a rejection of the claim that the assessment of practical teaching is an extremely inexact art, than a reluctance to yield up a power relationship. If that is the case it bodes ill for the future of supervision.

Blumberg (1974) discusses the perceptions held by various participants of supervision and refers to what he describes as 'disturbing and neglected findings' (pp.12ff.). These findings are from various investigations of supervisors' and supervisees' views on supervision. The picture that emerges is one that indicates that many of the teachers thought that supervision was a complete waste of time. The majority thought that supervision was part of the system that exists but plays no important function in their professional lives: it is seen as an irrelevant organizational ritual. Yates (1981) found similar attitudes in England. Student teachers and co-operating teachers thought supervisors less help to students than the co-operating teachers. Students thought the key aspect of the supervisors' role was that of assessment. At the same time they also thought the assessment of the co-operating teacher more valid than that of the supervisor. However, training institutions consider their assessments of student teaching to be more important than that of the schools, a finding which squares with those of Stones and Morris (1972a) and is implicit in the survey carried out by McCulloch (1979). Certainly the prevailing practice in arriving at the final assessment of student teachers in Britain is to 'take co-operating teachers' views into account' but for the decision to be made by the training institutions. The attitudes implicit in this practice are all of a piece with those referred to earlier and bespeak a complacency *vis à vis* the problems of assessment that sorts ill with the findings of the investigations discussed above.

Blumberg (1977), along with most of the authors referred to above, raises another problem inherent in assessment by supervisor. It is that of the conflict between the aspect of the role concerned with guidance and the aspect concerned with assessment. He argues that it is hypocritical and dishonest for a supervisor to collaborate with a teacher in interpersonal effort to improve the teacher's performance and then to fail the teacher for not succeeding. He believes that there is no place in supervision for assessment and that if it were ended forthwith there would be no more incompetent teachers in schools than there are at the moment. Lucio and McNeil (1969), looking at the question from an administrator's point of view, take a different approach and consider assessment as a vital part of a supervisor's role. However, they see assessment as subserving the task of teacher improvement. They are, of course, writing about American practice and are discussing the supervision of practising teachers. In fact the distance between this position and that of Blumberg's and mine is not as great as might appear at first sight. The removal of assessment from supervision does not imply that supervisors do not draw attention to student teachers' shortcomings as they perceive them, but that the threat implicit in assessment for certification or continued tenure is removed. Non-threatening advice is more likely to be heeded than advice given under threat of sanctions which will probably evoke attempts at impression management (Shipman 1967, Stones and Morris 1972b, Goldhammer *et al.* 1980, Sorenson 1967). Students and teachers who resist feedback given in a non-evaluatory colleaguial relationship, and insist on 'withering on the vine' as Lucio and McNeil put it, have problems other than pedagogical ones and action other than threats of failure is indicated.

The conflict between the helping and the evaluatory roles in supervision is rooted in history in Britain and elsewhere (Ryan 1971). The apprenticeship model of teacher education leave the acquisition of teaching skills to the imitative capabilities of the student and the luck of the draw in the allocation of the co-operating model teacher. There is nothing else to it. And, of course, the college supervisor is a late arrival on the scene in teacher education. The inspector, on the other hand, has been around for much longer, practically since popular education began to make demands for a corps of professional teachers. Thus inspection and assessment were well entrenched long before the idea of helping student teachers developed. And even when institutions for teacher training were established and helping students to become teachers became one of their accepted functions, the apprenticeship approach to training persisted and, indeed, is with us to this day.

Recent developments in the conceptualizing of evaluation bear on the problem of role conflict of this type. Conventional approaches to the assessment of student teaching lean heavily towards what has come to be called *summative* evaluation. Such evaluation implies once and for all final judgement. *Formative* evaluation, on the other hand, emphasizes growth and development (Sergiovanni and Starratt 1979). Formative evaluation also implies analysis and diagnosis, and I prefer the term *diagnostic evaluation*. Analysis of current performance makes possible the identification of strengths and weaknesses, a precondition for the enhancement of the former and the elimination of the latter. The helping function of supervision is to provide the conditions for this enhancement of performance. But since diagnostic evaluation is never ending, a key aspect of the supervisor's task is to help students to develop skills of diagnosis in respect of their own performance, so that when they leave college they will be capable of self-monitoring and improvement (Goldhammer *et al.* 1980, Stones 1979, Lanier 1981, Anderson 1972, Blumberg 1977).

Recognizing the inherent conflict between the helping and evaluatory aspects of supervision, some authors have argued for their separation and allocation to different people (Cogan 1976, Mickler 1972). Although this separation would not deal with the problem raised earlier, of the questionable validity of any current methods of assessment, so long as they persist separation could well be a useful intermediate step. Partington (1982) investigated a system of supervision in which teachers in schools acted as supervisors. He found that anxiety related to assessment, which was still the province of the university supervisor, was reduced.

Lanier (1981) was taking a futuristic view when she alluded to teacher self-assessment. At the moment, I suggest, we could well be on the verge of a transition from the apprenticeship mode of teacher preparation to one in which supervisors bring to bear a variety of information and practices that will break into the circle and clear the way towards that future.

The apprentice teacher

SITTING WITH NELLIE

However most current approaches to supervision adhere faithfully to past practice and show little sign of change. I suggest, therefore, that it is still appropriate to use the same sub-heading for this section as the one Sidney Morris and I adopted from industry in a book on practical teaching over a decade ago (Stones and Morris 1972b). We were referring to the approach to learning teaching by copying other teachers, the pedagogical analogue to the largely discredited industrial practice of inducting new workers by asking them to sit with an old hand. Essentially this approach implies a passive view of supervision since the neophyte teacher is expected to acquire teaching expertise by watching someone else teach and attempting to go away and do likewise. Given the nature of apprenticeship, the supervisor who attempts to take an active part is essentially an interloper interfering with the guidance of the master and his apprentice; the logic of the situation demands a passive role of the supervisor.

The passive approach is no doubt an important, if not the crucial factor identified in research into supervision which suggests that its effects are very limited. Morris (1974) found no difference between supervised students and non-supervised students either in performance or in adjustment. She concluded that other approaches to supervision should be developed and suggested some of the activities I turn to later which involve a more varied and active role for the supervisor. Bowman (1979) surveyed the evidence and concluded that supervision was ineffective and should be ended. He suggests that the job should be passed to 'master teachers' in distinction to Morris's proposals. Zimpher, deVoss and Nott (1980), while agreeing with the argument that supervision as it exists is ineffective, consider that it is simplistic to take this as a reason to abolish supervision. They argue that supervision is an extremely complex activity that certainly needs reconsideration, but towards changing not abolishing it. Hoste (1982), investigating the sources of influence on student teaching practice in a Scottish college, found that the students perceived the supervisor's influence as being minimal except in the field of assessment. Partington (1982) found that one of the important factors making for student preferences for school-based rather than university-based supervisors was the reduction of anxiety about assessment. The finding that students preferred this type of supervision is entirely consistent with the literature on students' attitudes to their training which almost invariably reports that they consider teaching practice the most useful aspect of their training. This is scarcely surprising in view of current conceptualizations of learning to teach as apprenticeship where the neophyte observes the master practitioner in action and attempts to do likewise.

On the strength of his investigation Partington implies that teacher training would be improved if supervision were to be school based. Stones (1977) takes a different view and argues that the way forward is to improve supervision through systematic study and experimentation, and describes a course intended to do that where supervisor training is seen as analogous to teacher training. This is not to suggest that the contribution of the class teacher is thereby devalued but that a different relationship between teacher, supervisor and student teacher and between pedagogical theory and practical teaching is necessary (Stones 1981, 1983). Cohn (1981) takes a similar line and describes an approach that involves methods akin to some of those I discussed in the papers of 1977, 1981 and 1982, and which I take up in greater detail below. The essential thrust of these articles is towards increased theory-based analytical approaches to supervision.

The same spirit informs the recent publication by Turney and others (1982a and b) of a major work in this field intended for use in Australia. The aim is the development of a comprehensive research-based set of guidelines of supervisor development. The published material comprises a book on the practicum in teacher education and a set of *role programmes* that goes into considerable detail about the nature of the activities in coping with the six *roles* seen as inherent to the tasks of supervisors. These *roles* comprise those of manager, counsellor, instructor, observer, feedback and evaluator. Information about and exercises related to the roles are provided in the hope that they will help supervisors to understand more clearly the aims and nature of their work, and to acquire the necessary skills in performing their roles.

Other writers (e.g. Mosher and Purpel 1972) have presented a somewhat different view of supervision in terms of 'models' with various objectives, i.e. the improvement of instruction, the enhancement of student teacher affect, and the enhancement of the student teacher's adjustment by and in group work with peers. Although the 'models' imply a more positive role for the supervisor than in the apprenticeship approach, I suggest that it is more appropriate to conceive of supervision as comprehending the key aspects of all the models in a unitary approach, and this is the line of argument I adopt in this book.

Supervision: video and small group work

An important step towards reconceptualizing the role of the supervisor occurred when microteaching using video feedback became possible. This development involved two key elements. Video recording enabled student teaching episodes to be preserved and available for discussion and repeated reinstatement, and the focusing on specific skills in microteaching concentrated supervisors' minds on the nature of satisfactory teaching in a way that global approaches to supervision had not done. The two do not necessarily coexist in individual supervisors' minds, however. Video recording is often used with traditional global approaches to supervision, and, of course, more analytical approaches are frequently found without video. But the two together hold the potential for changing fundamentally the role of the supervisor along the lines discussed in the previous section. They do not, however, guarantee change. The crucial thing that is all too frequently lacking is the pedagogical thinking that should inform the use of these techniques. Scrutiny of the literature, therefore, tends to yield somewhat limited insights into technical and instrumental matters rather than providing guidance towards a body of general theoretical principles.

The work of Borg *et al.* (1970) on the minicourse sees the use of video and structured teaching experiences as enabling teachers to assume responsibility for their own self-development without the need for supervisory involvement. They justify this approach by referring to experimentation that suggests that videotape self-evaluation and pupil feedback are superior to supervisor feedback. Non-American readers should remember, however, that this work refers to the American concept of supervision which commonly connotes the supervision of teachers in service and this applies to the minicourse. Fuller and Manning (1973), looking at findings of research in relation to the effects of video self-confrontation in teacher education, conclude that self-confrontation is more effective when complemented by supervisory comment focusing on critical aspects of the teaching. Other investigators come to the same conclusion (Peck and Tucker 1973). Griffiths (1975) provides a useful source of information about research on this question.

The lack of congruence in the literature in this field is more apparent than real and harks back to some of my earlier comments. It is not possible to talk about 'supervision' as if it were a homogeneous activity, a point alluded to in Griffiths's review. Comparing teacher development employing supervision with methods not using supervision is meaningless if one of the comparisons is based on an apprenticeship model and the other on supervision taking an analytical approach. Even within these two categories it is probably illegitimate to assume homogeneity when considering the effects of different approaches. It is therefore necessary to exercise caution when interpreting research findings, and to look upon work in the field as exploratory and continuing rather than definitive and conclusive.

Stones (1977, 1978b) discusses work of this nature in a course of supervisor training which uses video feedback for training supervisors in a common system of teacher training with students on initial training. Feedback here, however, is not seen as sufficient unto itself but as being integrally related to intervention by others, either peers or supervisors, in a shared context of pedagogical understandings. This work takes supervision to be a form of teaching and necessarily involves active intervention by the supervisor along the lines discussed by Fuller and Manning, but with the aim of enabling neophyte teachers to become quite independent of others and agents for their own development in a more fundamental way than that in Borg's minicourse. Further attention is given to this work later.

Among the factors that need attention when video feedback is employed in connection with supervision is the question of the 'cosmetic' reaction mentioned by Fuller and Manning. This is the tendency for most people to react to their early encounters with video feedback by attending to their appearance rather than to the nature of their teaching activity. It is allied to the problem of nervousness that most people feel on their first exposure to video recording. Some examples of reactions from teachers I have worked with are:

1 I felt an initial nervousness . . . later I was unaware of the camera for long periods of time. I was astonished how many nonverbal facial reactions and hand movements I made.

2 I was irritated by my tendency to stroke my moustache . . .
I was very conscious of the camera initially but although I
never forgot its presence, I soon stopped bothering about
it.

3 Initially I showed the usual signs of stage fright, licking
lips excessively, fidgeting with pen and holding myself in a
rigid sitting position.

These reactions are, perhaps, inevitable but need to be taken
into account when introducing CCTV into supervision. The
examples I have just quoted are typical of those I have found in
investigations of the attitudes of students on preservice and
inservice courses in teaching. With some people nervousness
can occasionally have quite severe effects and one of the
students on a course of postgraduate initial training among
those surveyed reported virtual paralysis. However, this particular case was complicated by the fact that the co-operating
teacher had asked the student to teach an aspect of marxist
philosophy to an unsophisticated group of pupils in one lesson;
a good illustration of the danger of drawing conclusions about
the cause-effect links when investigating the effects of different conditions of teaching and learning on supervisory
practice. Supervisors using video recording must also take into
account the effect of the use of the equipment on the pupils.
Nervousness might be a problem in small groups and when an
individual is picked out by the camera and there is the other
problem of pupils acting up to the camera. However, the
general finding in the literature on the use of recording
equipment in teaching seems to be that after a few exposures
teachers and pupils become less conscious of it. The message
seems to be that the more exposure pupils and teachers have to
video recording the less the problem will be. I discuss this
question and suggest ways of coping with it later.

Another problem I have encountered over many years but
which gets little mention in the literature is the technical/
production problem that goes with the use of hardware. I have
discussed the key points in various places (see Stones 1978b).
The problem is to ensure that the machinery is used for
pedagogical purposes and not to gratify the supervisor's, the
teacher's or the technicians' desire to play the professional television production team. A slick, dramatic, artistic,

68354

technically excellent production is *not* the aim of the exercise and this fact needs to be held firmly in mind by supervisors or they will be seduced without their knowing it. I attempt to cope with this difficulty by using unmanned equipment, an approach also discussed by Bailey (1979).

The other main feature of microteaching harks back to a practice that was common in British colleges under the heading of 'group practice'. In group practice a small number of students under the wing of one tutor visited schools and spent half a day or a day with classes of pupils. Individual students taught different lessons on the timetable under the eye of peers and tutor. Later the whole group would discuss the way the visit had gone so that students got feedback from peers and from the tutor on their teaching.

Microteaching, however, scales the operation down. It normally deals with less than a complete class, often around six pupils, and the sessions tend to be shorter than full lessons. But these are minor matters compared to the other difference between microteaching and group practice. The point I allude to is the practice of focusing on a specific 'teaching skill' (Allen and Ryan 1969). I suggest that this is particularly important because it breaks with the tradition of global appraisal of student teaching by supervisors and directs attention to the *teaching* rather than the *teacher*. Some of the skills that have attracted attention are such things as the use of reinforcement, questioning techniques, beginning a lesson, concluding a lesson and encouraging pupil participation. My own view is that although the skills approach to teacher induction was an important development it had a crucial weakness in that the selection of skills was *ad hoc* and unrelated to any pedagogical system (Stones 1981, 1983). That is, the skills for the most part comprise a collection of unrelated elements drawn from conventional teacher and supervisor beliefs and aspects of psychology. The effects of this lack of conceptual coherence related explicitly to pedagogical objectives may be observed by considering Rosenshine's (1971) review of the research linking teacher activities and pupil learning. One study he reviewed found a negative correlation between open questioning and pupil learning whereas what would be expected would be the reverse. Gall (1973) pointed out that when the nature of the test assessing the pupils' learning was taken into account there was no problem since the test was a simple test of rote learning and the teacher would have been better employed just drilling the pupils rather than 'wasting time' getting them to think.

This example underlines the general problem. Although many of the specific skills in microteaching were certainly derived from principles of human learning, when they began to be promulgated the principles were often interpreted mechanically. Asking probing questions was held to be a 'good thing' irrespective of the type of learning involved, whereas, although essential for complex conceptual learning, it is unnecessary for rote learning. Reinforcement is an important element in learning and certainly derives from a substantial body of theory, but unfortunately many schedules of guidance for specific skills training went no further than to list a few possible reinforcing teacher activities at the level of recipe knowledge – nodding, smiling, saying 'good'. Such activities would be useful in some conditions but disastrous in others. Students need the ability to decide on the best course of action in specific conditions not by remembering a list of 'reinforcers' or types of 'probing questions', but by rational thought based on previous experience and study. They cannot acquire this ability in brief encounters with their supervisor as they venture forth on teaching practice, it must be built into the course structure.

The crucial point, then, is that although we may take an analytical approach to teaching and involve students in discussions about specific aspects of their teaching, the different facets of their activity must be manifestations of deeper underlying capabilities that I refer to as the *deep structures* of teaching ability, not unrelated and *ad hoc* activities (Stones 1983). To achieve the state of affairs where specific student teacher action is the product of a unique and particular teaching situation and a deeply held grasp of theoretical principles, our conception of supervision must be one where student/supervisor relationship must be very different from today's staple. Thus for somewhat different reasons we come to the same point as that made by the various writers referred to earlier. That point is that unless the relationship between supervisor and supervised is one of trust and respect, the process of supervision is unlikely to achieve much. The baleful images of the supervisor/student relationship revealed in some of the investigations discussed above lead to student activities that reject or avoid the supervisor's intercession and render the whole procedure futile at best and more likely harmful.

Interpersonal relationships

Supervisors may have the best of intentions in approaching their tasks and still have problems because of their lack of awareness of the complexities of supervisor/student relationships. The literature on this question tends to focus on the interview that follows a piece of teaching and draws on work in the field of therapeutic counselling. The aim of this work is to elucidate the important aspects of the interactions and to sensitize counsellors to those aspects of counselling behaviour that are likely to enhance the effectiveness of the counselling. Social psychology literature is also a source of useful information to supervisors on key aspects of interpersonal perceptions.

Whitfield (1977) discusses what he considers the key element of positive interpersonal communication in a booklet of guidance to school supervisors. He takes the view that establishing positive interpersonal relations is primarily dependent upon nonverbal communication skills. He advances the following items as being of particular importance:

Eye contact and facial expression
Perceiving and responding with empathy
Perceiving and responding with warmth
Perceiving and responding with respect
Territoriality and spatial arrangement
Perceiving and responding in a non-threatening manner
Vocal intonation and inflexion
Gesturing
Perceiving and responding with concreteness
Using clarification skills.

These aspects of interpersonal relationships are a subset of a corpus of knowledge in the field of social psychology that deals with the psychology of dyadic exchanges (Argyle 1973). However, whereas the literature in social psychology tends to be descriptive, Whitfield's items are prescriptive in the sense of being suggestions to beginning teachers designed to draw on the findings of the psychology of interpersonal exchanges so as to enhance the effectiveness of the student/supervisor relationship. Boyan *et al.* (1973), in a handbook on the training of instructional supervisors, are prescriptive in the same sense. They also make the point that without an awareness of and competence in the skills of interpersonal interactions the supervisor's activity is likely to be ineffective. They refer to the primacy of the need to establish clear communication, understanding and mutual trust. They provide detailed information about the nature of interpersonal skills and exercises linked with the use of video materials to develop the skills in supervisors.

Acevedo *et al.* (1976) discuss various aspects of interpersonal interactions as they apply to supervision and provide exercises to improve them. They consider such things as establishing co-operative relationships, questioning techniques, nonverbal components of exchanges and listening skills to be important aspects of the relationship. Lang *et al.* (1975) consider the key aspects to comprise such things as listening, acceptance, openness, empathy and clarity. Hackney and Cormier (1979) provide a similar list from counselling therapy. They also go into detail about the elements of such things as counsellor reinforcing behaviour (nonverbal and verbal), opening and closing an interview and the process of relating to the interviewee. Although I do not wish to suggest that the supervisor/student relationship should be seen as therapeutic, I do believe that much of the theory and practice of counselling is applicable to that relationship. This is not unreasonable since both the approach to supervision being discussed here and counselling draw on psychological theories of interpersonal interaction. Thus specifics mentioned by Hackney and Cormier such as the maintaining of eye contact, the mirroring of affect, the use of body posture to encourage the interviewee, and the use of positive verbalizing are all highly relevant to satisfactory supervision.

The work of Ivey (1974a and b) and Gluckstern and Ivey (1975) makes a useful link between counselling, therapeutic procedures and the approach to be developed in later chapters. Ivey used microteaching techniques to train counsellors and other 'helpers and paraprofessionals'. Specific counselling skills are taught and video recordings used to provide the focus of discussion and to provide feedback. Ivey believes that the techniques he uses have wide application across the helping professions, and he specifically relates his work to training teachers in counselling skills so as to enhance their effectiveness (Ivey 1974a and b). I have taken a similar approach to the training of supervisors (Stones 1977). The important skills in Ivey's lexicon are similar to those discussed by the authors referred to earlier. For example attending behaviour has as its components: eye contact, physical posture, verbal following behaviour and listening skills. Ivey proposes four main groups of skills. Selective listening skills are the second dimension of what he refers to as microcounselling. This skill demands that one is sensitive and attends to emotional or feeling comments and key facial and bodily expressions. A third aspect is paraphrasing, that is the clear repetition of the essential content of another's comments. The fourth aspect is the skill of interpretation. This skill comprises analysis and restructuring meanings so as to help the client learn alternative views of reality.

In all, approximately a dozen component skills are derived from the four groups. I consider most of them are applicable to the supervisory interview following student teaching and essential to successful supervision, but I do not consider them sufficient. The important difference between the counselling interview and the supervisory interview is that the latter is part of a programme of activities with the objective of teaching students to teach. It is explicitly *teaching* but a complex form of teaching since its main focus should, I suggest, be on the theory and practice of pedagogy (Stones 1979, 1981, 1983). Therefore the techniques advocated by Ivey and the other exponents of a specific skills approach to counselling need to be augmented by the use by the supervisor of pedagogical skills in the act of teaching student teachers how they themselves can develop those pedagogical skills. Thus the Ivey approach to microcounselling is very valuable to *teachers* but needs to be complemented by pedagogical skills: *supervisor* skills demand this further dimension.

Pedagogical aspects

Unfortunately the study of pedagogy has been greatly neglected so that there is little in the literature to help either teachers or supervisors. Simon (1981) has discussed the historical reasons for this, and Smith (1980) and Stones (1978a, 1979, 1981, 1983) have argued for a much greater attention to pedagogy in teacher education and have drawn attention to the disjunction between theory and practice, especially in the field of educational psychology which should have a particular part to play in the development of teaching skills. Both Smith and Stones draw attention to the fact that supervisors very often have little knowledge of those aspects of learning theory that would be of value to student teachers. They argue that theory in courses of teacher preparation should be much more explicitly related to the practicalities of teaching. Supervisors should be the mediators between the theory and the practice, and if they do not themselves have a grasp of pedagogical theory they will not be able to help students develop their own pedagogical expertise, however much they may be able to help by the counselling skills discussed above.

We need to be careful, however, in considering the nature of the pedagogical theory. Unapplied or unappliable knowledge about learning theory will be no more use to the supervisor than it is to the teacher. This is a question seldom discussed in the literature on supervision, but an indication of the nature of the problem may be found in the *Handbook of Educational Supervision* (Marks *et al.* 1979). This book is intended as a practical guide for supervisors and covers a great many topics. However, pedagogy is not to be found in the index and learning theory gets no more than five-and-a-half pages out of the book's 699. The authors aver that, in order to be able to help teachers to improve instruction, supervisors must 'be aware of the basic principles concerning the learning process' (p.668). Unfortunately the learning theories they refer to are mainly those of psychologists of an earlier era whose work was generally concerned with animal learning and shows little acquaintance with recent developments in ideas about human learning and instruction. But another difficulty also very commonly found in courses of teacher training is that they present the information about the theories in global fashion with no analytical application to specific teaching problems. This is all of a piece with the way educational psychology is commonly taught by tutors in education and which is occasionally discussed in the literature on teacher training.

Clinefelter (1979), discussing 'educational psychology's identity crisis', argues that the literature in the field indicates a lack of precise definitions about curriculum, research emphases and accountability and that, to resolve the problems, educational psychologists should direct their attention to the classroom and the instructional processes that take place there. A survey carried out by Isakson and Ellsworth (1979) on a sample of seventy-seven American teachers reinforced this view, finding that the teachers were particularly interested in topics that bore on actual educational problems. Stones and Anderson (1972) reviewed the literature on the subject at that time and conducted a survey in the UK of the views of a large population of teachers, students and tutors, and came to much the same conclusion. Stones has subsequently developed the argument in papers on the application of psychology to pedagogy (Stones 1978a, 1979, 1981). However, despite the fairly extensive literature on the place of educational psychology in teacher education, a reasonable summary of the current situation would suggest that the precepts are honoured more than the practice. Theories of learning coexist with practical teaching but run on parallel lines in most teacher training institutions. Learning theories are held to be important for practical teaching, but connections are rarely explicated in specific teaching situations and frequently comprise descriptive accounts of the work of the psychologists currently in fashion. Student teachers learn about learning theory in the same way as they may learn about any other curriculum subject, as reception knowledge provided by transmission teaching, whereas it should be central to their theoretical and practical studies of teaching (Stones 1981, 1983).

As I suggested earlier the literature on supervision pays little attention to the subject of pedagogy or the application of learning theories. One of the problems is that since practically all the literature on the subject is American, *theory* quite often connotes the theory of administration and applies to the supervision of inservice teachers rather than the induction of beginning teachers. Another factor is that researchers and writers, not unreasonably, often make the counselling aspect the centre of their attention and seek for theoretical underpinnings for that. An example of this approach is Dussault's (1970) book on a theory of supervision in teacher education. This book expounds a Rogerian approach to supervision and relates student counselling to it. Lucio and McNeil (1969), within an administrative context, devote a chapter to learning theory. They say that learning theory should be *adapted* not *adopted* in supervision and suggest some guidelines for the supervisor, mostly from reinforcement theory. Lang *et al.* (1975) also enunciate principles from reinforcement theory and behaviour modification as of use in the act of supervision. On the other hand the book by Goldhammer *et al.* (1980) has little to say on the subject, nor has the recent book by Acheson and Gall (1980) which is intended as a guide to action for supervisors.

A reasonable synopsis of the current position in the way the literature on supervision treats of theory, and particularly pedagogical theory, would be as follows. Most texts that mention theory are likely to deal with theory of administration or those aspects of learning theories likely to be of use in the supervisory interview. These theories will probably be drawn in the main from the field of behaviour modification. Other theoretical notions will be drawn from interpersonal counselling, for example Rogerian theory. Few, if any, of the sources will be concerned to build into the counsellor/student relationship the deliberate and explicit use of principles from learning psychology that should provide the supervisor and the student with a common frame of pedagogical reference.

Clinical supervision

The development in supervision that seems to hold most promise for coping with the problems I have discussed above is *clinical supervision*. This is an approach that tackles supervision in an analytical and systematic way. This sharp focus on detail is the significance of the term *clinical*. It was developed in America in the 1950s and was subsequently adopted by many teacher training programmes. The books by Goldhammer *et al.* (1980) and Acheson and Gall (1980) describe the current status of, and provide guidance on, the use of clinical supervision. For a very useful conspectus on the subject Sullivan (1980) should be consulted. She provides an historical introduction and descriptive account of its key features. Briefly, clinical supervision aims to improve teaching and takes the view that teaching is a form of human behaviour that has structure and can be controlled. The teacher/supervisor relationship is seen as one of mutuality within a framework of respect for individual autonomy and self-regulated enquiry, analysis, examination and evaluation. It is not suggested that clinical supervision is a theory, but rather a model or set of procedures. These procedures are seen as a cycle of stages, the exact configuration of which differs somewhat from author to author although the general outlines are the same (Goldhammer *et al.* 1980, Mosher and Purpel 1972, Cogan 1976, Boyan *et al.* 1973).

Cogan's description may be taken as representative of the genre. He conceives of eight stages as follows:

1 Establishment of the supervisor/student relationship: explanation of the procedures and rationale.
2 Supervisor and student jointly plan lesson or series of lessons.
3 Supervisor and student jointly plan the arrangements for the observation of the teaching and collection of data about it.
4 Observation of teaching in classroom. Collection of data, possibly using some form of observation system (e.g. Flanders's system).
5 Student and supervisor analyse the teaching.
6 Planning the supervisory conference either by the supervisor alone or with the student.
7 The supervisory conference.
8 Planning for further teaching taking into account necessary changes.

Tests of the efficacy of the clinical model suggest it does, in fact, have some success in achieving its aims (Turner 1976). Teacher change occurred in line with the objectives (Krajewski 1976). Sullivan (1980), reviewing a number of doctoral dissertations on the subject of clinical supervision, reports a general finding of an increase in the teacher's self-confidence. Rapport and openness were found to be a particular feature of the approach.

There are strengths and weaknesses in clinical supervision. The criticisms levelled against conventional approaches by Blumberg, and the disquieting findings of other investigations discussed above concerning the nature of supervisor/student teacher interpersonal relationships, are largely answered and overcome when the model is implemented in the way it is promulgated. However, there may still be problems of role conflict that are not dealt with in the model as it is currently presented (Miller 1978). This may well be a consequence of the lack of clarity in the relationship between the supervisor and student, and may be a carry-over from the counselling field where the counsellor and client are sometimes seen as in a reciprocatory relationship of equals whereas in student teacher supervision this is patently not the case. There is also the problem I discussed earlier in connection with the literature on supervision generally, which is that it tends to focus on procedures and gives little attention to specific skills either in supervision or in teaching (Krajewski 1976).

This last point touches on my own main reservation. It is not, however, sins of commission in clinical supervision as it is presented by writers such as Goldhammer *et al.* that concern me, but rather the lack of clearly defined notions of the nature of the desired outcomes in terms of pupil learning and development. As I have argued above and as the main theme of this book expounds, we must go beyond procedures and cycles and develop the pedagogical underpinnings of the whole supervisory process. If we do not do something like this we may achieve good interpersonal relationships and highly satisfactory supervisory procedures but leave unaddressed the complex question of the theoretical premises about pupil learning upon which our counselling and guidance are based.

3

· · · · · · · · · ·

Aims and objectives

It is an interesting exercise to try to work backwards from a selection of schedules used for the assessment of practical teaching in British training institutions to induce the main aims of supervision. I am assuming, of course, that the schedules are intended to embody and encapsulate those aspects of teacher activities and attributes thought to be criterial for 'good' teaching. This seems a reasonable assumption since presumably the schedules were originally devised to assess the extent to which the student teachers fulfilled those criteria.

Such an exercise would not reveal all the objectives of supervision. However, it should give us a fair idea of their main elements since supervisors will, at least, be concerned to ensure that their students attain the objectives they, the supervisors, consider to be criterial of good teaching and at a level they think appropriate.

However, four recent analyses of schedules used in British institutions to assess competence in teaching suggest that it would be very difficult indeed to abstract from the array of specific criteria any clear idea of the general aims of teaching practice (Stones and Morris 1972a, Norris 1974, McCulloch 1979, Saunders and Saunders 1980). The reader is referred to the smörgasbörd of specific criteria laid out in McCulloch's report for a flavour of current fashion. Stones and Morris made an attempt and subjected the criteria they collected in their national survey to factor analysis, but found little evidence of conceptual coherence that might have pointed to any unifying overall aims. They considered that 'the conceptual strain involved in identifying the common elements in factors that sorted together such things as standard of lesson notes, use of aids, and appearance and dress was too much, and . . . that there was little evidence of conceptual unity in the factor analysis'. It would seem, therefore, that anyone seeking enlightenment about the overall purposes of supervision, by scrutinizing what are currently thought desirable activities for a student teacher on teaching practice, is likely to be disappointed. Should one consult specific schedules such as those set out in McCulloch's report the outcome will be similar. The picture one gets is of vagueness and heterogeneity that is of little help in orienting supervisors to their task.

Deriving objectives

I believe this vagueness and heterogeneity arises because there has never been any sustained systematic attempt to delineate the aims and objectives of practical teaching or the supervision of student teachers. Items related to assessment have accreted over the years and schedules have been cannibalized to make 'new' versions: compare the nineteenth-century schedule referred to in chapter one and contemporary instruments. Rarely is there any attempt to provide theoretical justification for the choice of items on assessment schedules. Indeed, it would be difficult to do this in the absence of a clearly defined overall rationale or superordinate objectives. The disparate elements may be amenable to some form of crude grouping but, as the investigations referred to above indicate, these groupings are more in the nature of fortuitous collections than logically or psychologically related concepts and principles.

I referred earlier to the fact that pupil learning is rarely included as an item in teacher assessment schedules. This omission is of great significance for supervisors. Is the reason for its neglect that pupil learning is not considered important? Is it neglected because it is too difficult to assess? Or because nobody thought about it? Or is it taken for granted that all the items on the schedules are subordinate contributory elements to a global evaluation of teaching competence that takes pupil learning as its acid test? If it is argued that the last proposition is the operative one, several difficult questions arise. The first is to ask why, if pupil learning is fundamental, do few, if any, schedules ever include an item on the assessment of pupil learning? Another question is, how do the items on the various schedules actually relate to effective pupil learning? Some, such as those concerning students' personal appearance, may have very tenuous and problematic connections. Others, such as those which ask whether the student can use the chalkboard, may have an unexplicated link that seems plausible but could well refer to activities which are only spuriously related to pupil learning.

I suspect that the reason for the neglect of pupil learning as a criterion of teacher assessment is an amalgam of the possibilities referred to. Pupil learning *is* difficult to assess except at the most trivial level. Pupil learning *has* undoubtedly been overlooked in the process of focusing on what the student teacher does or looks like. And descrying the links between currently emphasized criteria and effective pupil learning is a most complex operation.

This is not surprising. Attempting to find unifying concepts for collections that have arisen by eclectic accretion will stretch anyone's intellect and imagination with no guarantee of success. The most effective way of resolving the problems outlined is to come to some conclusion about the general aims of practical teaching and take this as the point of departure for explicating subordinate objectives that can be clearly seen as contributory to the main aims and offer guidance to supervisors in their attempts to help student teachers attain them.

An approach

The approach I propose is akin to that outlined in Stones and Anderson (1972). This is a taxonomic approach that proceeds analytically from the global aims to identify what are taken to be subordinate and specific objectives. The specific objectives are subordinate in a logical/hierarchical sense and also in the sense that they are essential to the achievement of the overall aims. For example, a knowledge of the optimum conditions for concept learning is logically subsumed under the overall aim of teaching for effective learning, and it is an essential prerequisite for a teacher hoping to help pupils to learn effectively.

There are several advantages in an approach of this type. One is that by proceeding from the most general to the most particular *and making the objectives explicit as one proceeds* it is possible to identify the degree of consensus about the objectives and where it breaks down. Every supervisor would agree that one of the main aims of supervision is to produce competent teachers. Strains are likely to appear, however, as soon as this general statement is subjected to analysis by asking questions that probe the understanding different people have of it. Until this kind of examination is carried out it is highly probable that the generally agreed statement will embody a spurious consensus in which different people have very different ideas about the nature of the phenomenon under scrutiny. Unless it is carried out supervisors will be comfortable in the cosy consensus but there is little chance of significant progress in teacher preparation.

Another very important aspect of this approach to identifying the objectives of supervision is that it provides touchstones by which specific items related to the assessment of teaching can be tested for their likely contribution to the success of the supervisor's actions. With the current heterogeneous collections of criteria thought to be important for successful teaching, each criterion, were it to be questioned, would need its own justification. This applies when attempts are made to group criteria since the generic titles of the groupings are often labels of convenience rather than accurate descriptions that bring phenomena together because of their conceptual coherence. Scrutiny of practically any schedule for the assessment of teaching will yield examples of this heterogeneous grouping. For a specific source of examples see Appendix X in McCulloch 1979.

The adoption of an approach of this type, coupled with a conviction that children's learning should be considered the overriding aim of teaching, helps considerably in the elucidation of the aims of supervision. The overall aim of supervision may then be seen as guiding student teachers in their learning how best to optimize pupil learning. The fact that the supervisor's aim *vis à vis* student teachers is the same as the student teacher's *vis à vis* the pupils is of profound significance for the way supervision is conceived and operationalized. It holds the potential for providing a common frame of pedagogical reference for the teaching and learning of pupils, student teachers and supervisors, a theme to which we shall return frequently during the course of our consideration of the nature of supervision.

The enunciation of this overall aim and proposed mode of proceeding may be a help but it does not solve all the problems. A key question that immediately arises is to ask what is implied when we talk about 'learning' as applied to pupils or student teachers. However, the adoption of an analytical approach such as I suggest is a useful heuristic device that helps to make the matter explicit to supervisors and their peers. This not only makes clear the attitudes and values embodied in the overall statement but provides a way of identifying more precisely the nature of the supervisor activities necessary to achieve the aims.

To amplify this point. There is a view of 'learning' that sees it as evidenced when pupils have acquired the ability to recite catechismally what they have previously been drilled in, for example, the dates of dynasties or multiplication tables. There is another view that takes as evidence the ability to answer three-hour examination papers in which students rehearse arguments their tutors have previously promulgated, a mode which is probably a higher form of catechism. Other examples may relate to the acquisition of motor skills or of obedience to teachers' instructions. Examples of these approaches to learning can be seen in profusion in schools today. And not only in schools but also in courses aimed to teach teaching, as I suggested in earlier chapters. Much less in evidence is an approach that aims at learning that will enable pupils and student teachers to solve problems. In my view this should be the crucial type of learning that student teachers and supervisors should be engaged in.

A common pedagogy

The approach that I espouse sees the learning of the pupil, the student teacher *and the supervisor* as enquiry-oriented. The idea of enquiry-oriented learning is a complex one demanding more detailed consideration than I can give here. I have, however, written at greater length and in detail about this approach in *Psychology of Education: A Pedagogical Approach* (Stones 1979). Its salient characteristics may be briefly described but should be regarded as no more than a broad indication of a complex phenomenon.

This type of learning is pre-eminently about problem solving and transferability. That is, learners are not primarily concerned with learning 'facts' but with acquiring skills that will equip them to operate adaptively in a wide variety of situations. Learning facts may be a necessary part of this type of learning but only to the extent that it facilitates the more complex learning. Thus children's learning will equip them to cope effectively with solving problems in the field in which they are working at any one time. Student teachers' learning will equip them to solve pedagogical problems in a variety of teaching situations through a grasp of some general principles of teaching that transcend the teaching of specific subjects to specific groups of pupils. Supervisors themselves will also be involved, perhaps in a rather different way, but subject to the same learning processes.

Enquiry is a factor common to all three groups of learners. Pupils investigate the applicability of new skills, acquired with the guidance of teachers, to solving new problems. Student teachers test the effectiveness of the skills their supervisors have helped them to acquire in guiding pupils' learning. Supervisors themselves explore the validity of their theory and practice by observing the extent to which they produce adequate pupil and student teacher ability to do the same. This approach bespeaks an open-ended view of learning that is never complete, that is always subject to further development and refinement by a continuous testing of theory against practice. It is an approach that unifies the activity of all actors in the processes of learning, teaching and supervision.

Elements of enquiry

This approach to identifying objectives, and the view of learning as enquiry, provide an orientation towards desirable supervisor activities at different levels of specificity. Key activities in the psychomotor and cognitive fields would be aimed at the development in student teachers of the ability to teach pupils to solve problems in a variety of subjects. Key affective activities would be aimed at developing in the student teachers a commitment to encouraging pupils to learn in this way effectively and with pleasure. These supervisor activities are not really separable; together they imply a central objective of supervision as the development in the student teacher of a competence in and commitment to independent pedagogical problem solving. It is important to stress the *independent* aspect of this statement. Unless this objective is achieved student teachers are not properly equipped for the profession.

The adoption of objectives such as these by supervisors clearly has profound significance for the way they approach their task. It implies a value position committed to respecting the autonomy of the student teacher and of the pupil. There can be no question of tutors dispensing information or tips for teachers in an *ex cathedra* mode. There can be no appeal to an arcane inner mystique to justify comments on students' teaching such as I have seen on videotape of a supervisor's reviewing a lesson with a student teacher. In the course of an unbroken monologue of about fifteen minutes the supervisor, making a critical comment, justifies his remarks by saying that his 'teaching mind' tells him that her action was wrong. Such an approach negates the idea of autonomy and independence and cannot possibly help students to acquire the understanding and skills necessary to solve pedagogical problems. The objectives I am proposing preclude this type of approach. The supervisor I have in mind is the one Blumberg's teachers had in mind when they described the supervisor of the future.

Apart from questions of values, teaching student teachers to solve pedagogical problems independently is not to be achieved by an *ex cathedra* pedagogy. It is not merely a question of tutors' practising what they preach. Problem solving simply cannot be taught expositorily. The supervisor approach most likely to achieve this objective is one in which the student teacher, the supervisor and the co-operating teacher in the school when possible, are all explicitly engaged in a joint problem-solving activity whose aim is to help the students teach effectively. This cannot be done unless the participants share a common field of discourse that replaces appeals to authority and experience to substantiate supervisors' assertions.

The identification of that common field of discourse provides a further pointer towards the objectives of supervision. Since the student teachers' aim is to become self-directed teachers, able to help children learn effectively, it is incumbent on supervisors to introduce students to theoretical principles that will assist them in their tasks. I believe that these principles are most likely to be found in the literature on psychology and human learning. I also believe that although there is very much work still to be done in this field, there is far more useful information about the way humans learn that is often realized by teacher educators. I have explored this field in depth and extensively elsewhere (Stones 1979, Stones and Anderson 1972) but a synoptic overview may point to the nature of the objectives that constitute the elements of enquiry I alluded to above.

With the overall objectives I have enunciated, subordinate objectives may be derived by analysis of their constituent elements. I suggest that four key areas of learning psychology hold promise for the achievement of those objectives. The most obvious contribution is clearly that derived from studies of problem solving in humans and especially those that accentuate the way in which intervention by others can enhance the process, both as to speed and elegance of solution. Contributory to this aim is the need for an objective that demands that student teachers acquire an understanding of how humans learn concepts and how they can be helped to do so. Concept learning should be one of the prime aims of most teachers. It constitutes the *content* of lessons. All too often, however, teachers do not understand the principles of concept learning or the ways in which teachers can intervene to speed up the process and ensure that the pupils do in fact learn the concepts *and not just the words.* Yet problem solving ability is greatly dependent upon the possession of a suitably extensive body of concepts in the appropriate field. An objective that student teachers acquire a thorough understanding of concept learning is vital for successful teaching.

Another key objective for student teacher learning is that they acquire the ability to make use, in their teaching, of information from the study of the way humans learn physical skills. I am not here alluding only to skills in the field of arts and crafts and physical education. There are many skills that, if not learned or learned inefficiently, can cause pupils serious problems in all their work. One thinks of such things as handwriting or simple sketching. There is information from the psychology of skill learning that will help student teachers to cope more effectively in this field. However, in most cases of skill teaching the teacher will probably know nothing of the psychology of skill learning and will probably use the 'show and tell' method, i.e. teacher demonstrates and asks the pupils to do likewise. This approach is of doubtful efficacy and is more likely to impede learning than enhance it. To take a ubiquitous example of this problem consider the case of teaching handwriting. Very often teachers will demonstrate the formation of letters and the action of the hand on the chalkboard. Writing on the chalkboard is a very different skill from writing on paper, as the student teachers are themselves discovering. Further, what is often being demonstrated is not the skill itself, but the finished product of the exercise of the skill. Even if the pupils could faithfully copy the teacher they would be learning the wrong actions. This is but one example off a very widespread phenomenon in teaching that is in urgent need of systematic study and application by teachers.

One objective contributory to the overall aim pervades all teaching. I refer to the motivation of the learner. There must be an objective that demands that student teachers acquire a deep understanding of those aspects of learning psychology that shed light on motivation and the reinforcement of learning. Without high motivation and reinforcement pupils will not learn effectively at any level. I am well aware that in many courses in training institutions, much attention is devoted to the subject of motivation in lectures and seminar discussions. Sadly, the discussion and lectures are often removed from reality and 'academic' in the worst sense. What is sorely needed is the consideration by student teachers of current information on the subject that can actually be applied to real learners in real teaching situations. Lacking this kind of information, anything they learn in training is likely to be inert knowledge and of little use in practical teaching. This is a fact of life that supervisors will need to bear in mind.

My suggested adoption of these objectives as elements of the overall objective illustrates an important point. They are not illustrative of a particular psychological persuasion. The approach is pluralistic. Those aspects of learning psychology that have demonstrated efficacy in explaining and enhancing human learning have been drawn on whatever school of thought they are believed to espouse. This point is important because all too often teachers and tutors have rejected systematic approaches to teaching because they are seen as belonging to a school of thought with which they are out of sympathy. Reinforcement theory is a particularly troublesome area. All too often it is explicitly rejected because of its largely imagined non-human nature whilst being implicitly and unconsciously misapplied in practice. Explicating the nature of the various approaches to the psychology of human learning and teaching is the essential first step in a considered adoption or rejection of their principles.

Subsequent steps involve the identification of objectives contributory to the overall ones. For example, the analysis of the elements of concept learning points to the need for student teachers to be able to identify and produce exemplars and possibly non-exemplars of concepts and, particularly important, to be able to present graded series of exemplars so as to maximize pupil learning of the concepts. Information on these subjects is available in the literature and can be consulted by student and supervisor as part of the exploration of a practical teaching task.

The same procedure applies to the other aspects of human learning that I outlined above but there is a further fundamental aspect of the procedure that affects profoundly the nature of the student/supervisor relationship. It is the point I referred to earlier, that in the main supervisors' objectives are virtually the same as students' objectives. Take the case just mentioned of concept learning. Supervisors will need to take into account the principles of concept learning they are trying to teach pupils *in their own teaching of students.* We are here in a sort of pedagogical Chinese box: it can get a bit confusing at times but it has its advantages. Because supervisors and students are both teaching they are attempting to make connections between the same body of theoretical principles and a practical teaching interaction. Of course the practical teaching situations are different. Factors relating to group and social learning apply to student teachers' teaching activity while factors relating to dyadic learning characterize supervisors' teaching. The common unifying factor, however, that both are concerned with similar kinds of human learning, outweighs the differences and provides that common field of pedagogical discourse that is so important for the students' learning and the supervisor/student relationship.

An example of this common pedagogy, which frequently arises in supervisor counselling sessions with student teachers, is the joint reference to ideas of concept teaching to illuminate the nature of the students' own learning as well as that of their pupils. In such discussions, students come to understand how their own learning of a concept, such as good teaching, depends, among other things, on the supervisor providing them with a suitably selected number of exemplars, stressing the attributes considered to be criterial, in exactly the same way as they would operate when teaching specific concepts to pupils.

I do not propose to go any further in my delineation of objectives: that is a matter for another book, and, in fact, is spelled out in Stones 1979. The salient point about the procedure, however, is that having adopted the overall aim one then proceeds to tease out the subordinate elements. In the process of analysis one declares one's attitudes and values by the choices one makes of the subordinate objectives. In my case I have taken the enhancement of pupil learning as a central aim in all teaching and the enhancement of student teacher learning as the central aim of supervisor activity. In both cases I am taking the broad view of learning I proposed above, a view that embraces the emotional and attitudinal as well as the cognitive. From those choices flow my decisions to focus on theory of learning as providing the common field of discourse for supervisor and student teacher and, in conjunction with the practical experience of the classroom, a pedagogical network that embraces all participants.

It will not have escaped the reader's attention that the objectives suggested above bespeak a view of supervision somewhat at odds with the way things are now in many training institutions. Instead of courses in the 'education disciplines' and 'practical teaching', the argument is for a unified pedagogy involving theory and practice of teaching and learning. The overall aim of the course is the production of teachers who are skilled practitioners in an art and science of a teaching that is theory based, enquiry-oriented and self-monitoring. I hasten to add that I am *not* suggesting that we ignore the study of the subject disciplines, or of the ecology of the school and classroom, and this approach will demand the application of educational studies to problems of teaching and being a teacher. I am suggesting that a reconceptualizing of the nature of teaching practice and its relationship to theory is of vital importance. I am suggesting that the aims and objectives of supervision should not be concerned exclusively with the practical work of students in classrooms, but also with the theory without which that practice is blind.

It would be foolish to ignore the practical problems posed by the adoption of an approach to supervision of this kind. Staff of training institutions nurtured in a very different environment may well feel diffident about attempting it, even if they accept its validity and value. Programmes of staff development are clearly one way of overcoming the problems but are likely to be difficult to come by. A bootstrap operation is not out of the question provided that supervisors are sufficiently motivated to explore the literature and experiment. I discuss possible approaches to inservice courses and bootstrap operations in later chapters.

Supervisor effectiveness

The assessment of supervisor effectiveness is as difficult as it is rare. I have already suggested that the assessment of pupil learning presents problems of a complexity almost invariably unappreciated by teachers. But the adoption of pupil learning as *the* criterion of successful teaching demands that considerable importance be attached to its effective assessment. However, we are particularly concerned here with the achievement of supervisors' objectives and this adds another dimension to the problem. Supervisors will have achieved their objectives if students achieve theirs and produce successful learning in pupils. Thus any schedule or checklist for the evaluation of student teaching should have as an important element the assessment of pupil learning, including affective aspects. On this criterion virtually all schedules currently in use are non-starters. As to schedules relating to supervisor effectiveness they are virtually non-existent. I outline a schedule in a later chapter intended as a heuristic guide to supervisor action that resembles an assessment instrument and at the same time raises an interesting and important question for assessment. It is: should we take the assessment of the ultimate goal of teaching and supervision, i.e. pupil and student learning, as the only criterial element in assessment, or should we take into account the teaching activities we believe are essential to successful pupil or student teacher learning? In the case of assessment of student teacher effectiveness the evaluation of competence would in the latter case include those actions that gave evidence of the students' understanding of principles of human learning as well as the learning outcomes of the pupils.

It seems to me that it is crucial to include the appraisal of these contributory elements in the overall assessment. This follows from the view of supervision I am suggesting. Conventional assessment is primarily concerned with categorizing students and rarely serves a useful pedagogical function. The assessment I am concerned with here is assessment of the supervisor as much as of the student. If students do not demonstrate competence supervisors need to know why so that they can take remedial action. Assessment is not now concerned with categorization but with diagnosis and remediation. The important difference is that with the former the responsibility for student teacher success or failure is entirely with students, with the latter supervisors assume the responsibility and seek information that will be useful in helping students overcome their deficiencies. This approach is one that supervisors will foster in their students so that it can hardly be inappropriate for their own work.

There is an implication for supervisory objectives in this discussion of assessment. It will be important to include the acquiring of skills in the assessing of learning by student teachers in those objectives. I am not suggesting a simple approach to writing and marking tests, but the cultivation of an understanding of the theory and practice of the evaluation of different forms of learning that will equip students to assess their pupils' progress and identify the important features of success and failure as a guide to remedial activity. In fact, evaluation of learning should be a built-in feature of the objectives I discussed earlier, and it could well be argued that it is an indispensable part of them.

Objectives and action

The specifying of objectives for supervision commits one to a particular value system since one chooses from a universe of possible goals. One is also thereby committed to certain ways of working when one seeks to achieve the objectives. Thus the enunciation of an overall goal that aims to produce teachers who are independent pedagogical problem solvers implies an approach to supervision that respects the autonomy of students and aims at a mode of supervisor/student interaction that will foster students' independence. However, the more detailed spelling-out of quite specific objectives does not dictate to the supervisor the precise means whereby the objectives must be achieved. The destination may be a generally agreed common one, but decisions about the mode of reaching the goal are personal to the supervisor. It is a question of strategy and tactics. But obviously supervisors' modes of operation are unlikely to be quirkily idiosyncratic if they are drawing on common bodies of theory. In the discussions that follow I explore ways in which supervisors might achieve the objectives proposed in this chapter through personal implementation of some of the approaches found to be helpful by a variety of teacher educators. And even those who may have reservations about some of the objectives might well find the modes of proceeding of value.

4

Pedagogical skills

The commitment to the goals enunciated in the previous chapter implies the need to identify the type of teacher activity most likely to foster pupils' ability to solve problems in novel situations. Since teachers cannot predict all possible situations with which their pupils are likely to be faced, the pedagogical skills that *teachers* need should be appropriate to the development in *pupils* of abilities of general application. Thus the skills should not be concerned with pupils' acquiring highly specific competencies, nor should they treat in a superficial way the acquisition of general capabilities. It is also important that the skills focused on are genuinely criterial to pupil learning.

The last point is important because many skills focused on at present, although useful on occasion in helping pupils to learn, are not essential. Sometimes these skills receive considerable attention, to the neglect of skills that *are* essential. A plausible reason for this, in my opinion, is that the former are readily identifiable and simple to deal with whereas the latter are often poorly understood and very difficult to deal with. A common example of the former type of skill is that favourite of teacher assessment schedules: 'Can the student (teacher) use the blackboard?' (McCulloch 1979, Appendix X). In certain circumstances it may be very useful to be able to use the chalkboard, but it is by no means essential to be able to do so. There are, indeed, many circumstances where it would be deleterious. For example, if a teacher wrote wrong information. A more pervasive example is the widespread use of chalkboards for writing or drawing material for pupils to copy into their notebooks. The most beautiful blackboard writing and drawing is positively harmful if it is factually or pedagogically rubbish. On the other hand there are teaching skills that are so fundamental that they enable teachers to decide when it is appropriate to use a chalkboard and when not. Teachers with these skills will also realize that chalkboards are just one among many ways of presenting information that may be contributory to pupil learning. Whether they do have this understanding has nothing to do with the teachers' ability to use the chalkboard but whether they have the necessary pedagogical skills to make use of it so that pupils will learn satisfactorily.

From the supervisor's point of view, the focusing on non-essential skills, or on the surface manifestations of basically essential skills, may give a misleading impression of the student's competence. A scintillating verbal display or beautifully produced AVA, or even the liberal use of standard 'reinforcers', could impress and distract and conceal a basic pedagogical poverty in the teaching. The use of heuristic guides, such as we consider later, helps one to attend to the pedagogical basics and ensures that the fundamental aspects of the teaching are taken into account. The key criterion, of course, is whether or not the pupils learned what the student was attempting to teach them. But, of course, in order to gain any inkling into which student activities produced, or did not produce, pupils' learning, it is necessary for the supervisor to ensure that all aspects of relevant teacher activities are attended to and not just the attractive surface ones.

Teaching skills: basic or surface?

To illustrate my point I should like to draw on a distinction I have made between my view of pedagogical skills and what is commonly implied when skills are referred to in other educational contexts such as, for example, microteaching. First I stress that the phrase refers to complex cognitive activities not merely simple motor activities. Second, and of particular importance, I view them as the *deep structures* of teaching ability (with acknowledgements to N. Chomsky). They consti- tute the underlying grasp of principles by teachers, and their practical application lies in helping pupils to learn by teacher's deployment of a variety of *surface* activities, i.e. teaching methods. Thus teachers with an understanding of these deep structures would manifest them in the way most appropriate to a specific teaching situation. Since every lesson must of necessity be unique, given the complexity of the interactions of human beings in different relationships, and the complexity of the abstractions inherent in these interactions, every approach to teaching must of necessity also be unique. Thus equipping a student teacher with highly specific 'tips' might work in some conditions but could be disastrous in others. The implementation of a teaching plan, and its consequent interactions based on a grasp of a body of general principles, will equip students to take into account the nature of the uniqueness of the specific situation and provide guidance about the necessary appropriate action.

It is sometimes argued that our knowledge of theoretical principles relevant to teaching is not sufficiently developed to be useful to student teachers. Yet there is a fairly substantial body of knowledge about human learning. What have been lacking are systematic attempts to apply this knowledge to teaching. Indeed, as I suggested earlier, much of the work in training institutions has focused on teaching student teachers *about* learning theory rather than exploring ways of trying it in practical teaching activities. Conventionally student teachers have been introduced to various 'schools' of theorists by transmission methods and often invited to come to their own conclusions about the veridicality of the theories. It is also widely averred that students will see the relevance to teaching of what they have been told when they have been out in the field for a few years.

An extreme example of this approach may be found in the *Handbook of Educational Supervision* (Marks *et al.* 1979). At the end of a book of some 699 pages of guidance to supervisors, the authors cover child development and the principles of educational psychology in fourteen pages, and of these, six pages are devoted to 'Psychology of the learning process for supervisors'. The authorities presented as relevant are Koffka, Koehler, Lewin, Wheeler, Robinson, Dewey, Thorndike, Guthrie, Hull, Skinner and Tolman, and a few lines are devoted to the authors' interpretation of their views. A final comment reads: 'It is the job of the supervisor to help the teacher become increasingly familiar with the more basic teachings of the psychologists in the field of learning.'

I have referred to this approach to learning theory as galloping through the gurus (Stones 1981). And, although British training institutions may have a less musty selection than the one just mentioned, the principle is the same. Courses of teacher training present students with massive compendia of tips and homilies capped with ludicrously truncated and oversimplified descriptions of the views of currently fashionable theorists in various fields, including learning psychology. Instead of interrogating psychology to gain insight into pedagogical processes, student teachers memorize a sterile catechism of sayings of the psychological sages for reasons that rarely have anything to do with the development of teaching skills.

Yet psychology is there to be interrogated, and should be. Further, I would argue that it is an essential part of supervisors' work to do that interrogating in co-operation with their students. And when they come to explore the relationship between the formulations of authorities in the field of human learning and the actual working-out in practical teaching, the approach should be experimental and investigatory, and explicitly seek to test the relevance of given theoretical formulations to pedagogical practice.

In subsequent chapters I expand upon this theme. However, I think it might be helpful to stress here that the joint explorations I refer to propose not only a new approach to supervision, but also the reappraisal of current views on pedagogy. The learning that supervisor and student should be concerned with goes beyond the low level rote learning so currently prevalent and both can obtain guidance from the principles of learning psychology. There is almost certainly a problem here in respect of practical teaching. That is, because of the past neglect of the study of meaningful learning in school contexts, teachers and student may well not perceive there to be any difficulty, since they equate teaching with telling. I suggest that a key aspect of the supervisor's task is to lead students to the realization that teaching should not be like that, and that rather teaching is a complex problem-solving activity that never ends. Teachers are in schools to solve problems. The most important problem they face is how best to help children to learn meaningfully. I suggest the kind of teaching they should be concentrating on is teaching pupils to solve problems for the reasons I outlined earlier. Supervisors also have their problems, and although they are not the same as those of pupils or teachers there are many important common factors so that supervisor, student teacher, pupil and any co-operating teacher share a common pedagogical preoccupation.

Skills: co-operative exploration

The idea of the different participants in the process of student teaching being involved in the same web of learning harks back to the last chapter. There I suggested that the relationship between supervisor and student teacher ought to be of a reciprocal nature, as they address the problem of improving student teaching. The suggestion was not merely a reflection of a wishy-washy liberal ideological outlook but a belief that the best hope of students' learning to solve pedagogical problems lies in their grappling with them in real teaching situations, with the co-operative guidance of supervisors. There is little if any chance of students learning to solve these problems through tutors lecturing them on problem solving or through supervisors passing *ex cathedra, ad hoc* comments on specific acts of teaching.

The logic of this argument supports the view implicit in the opening remarks of this chapter, that student teachers should be acquainted with as much as possible of the corpus of knowledge about effective ways of problem solving by human beings in so far as it is relatable to their teaching. I am not suggesting an historical parade of the views of various 'schools' of psychological thought about how various types of animals and humans solve problems. What I am suggesting is an attempt to identify those aspects of learning psychology, of whatever persuasion, that offer promise of guidance towards intervening in the process to enhance problem solving.

The approach suggested, then, is pluralist and interventionist. Pluralist in the sense that it holds no purist allegiance to one school of thought, and interventionist in that it is preoccupied with teacher action rather than observation. And in view of the key place of supervisors in the teaching/learning complex, their action is crucial. Their intervention is the pedagogical wellspring that nurtures the growth of student teachers and pupils. It is therefore incumbent upon supervisors to introduce students to principles from learning theory that appear relatable to the teaching of problem solving, and to work with them in exploring the applicability of principles to real practical teaching.

Exploration is the operative word. Work in learning psychology has rarely ventured into classrooms so that attempts by teachers to employ promising approaches are frequently ventures into genuinely new territory, even though the general terrain may be to some extent familiar. Thus supervisors will not be in a position to hand down to students recipes for them to follow to produce the learning of useful ways of tackling particular teaching problems, even if this was their favoured way of operating. Rather they will have to explore with students in specific and concrete teaching activities the actual working-out of general theoretical principles. The teaching activities of supervisors will thus also be learning activities for them as well as their students.

I do not wish to suggest that every lesson is to be a shot in the dark for student and supervisor. Far from it. The theoretical principles are genuine guides to action but they can only provide heuristic guides not algorithms. Individual teachers will work out their own particular modes of operating, drawing on the general principle. Students' and supervisors' learning results from this heuristic exploration and I do not think it too fanciful to suppose that this informed investigation will in time add to our understanding of the general principles.

Heuristics in skill learning

I have made a personal attempt to provide a heuristic for student teacher problem solving in which I bring together some of the formulations from learning psychology that seem to offer promise for pedagogy (Stones 1979). There is little new in the individual elements in the heuristic but the unifying of the various items in a schedule of guidance to teaching action is novel. It would not be possible to discuss the heuristic on problem solving here since it takes up a whole chapter in the original and the reader is referred there for details. The important thing, however, is not the detail of the heuristic schedule but its rationale and significance for supervisors.

All the schedules in the book were, in fact, developed for use by supervisors. Although to some extent they resemble the schedules for the assessment of teaching practice, they are actually quite different in rationale. Unlike teaching practice assessment schedules, they are intended as preactive guides to action, rather than checklists of points related to teacher assessment during or after teaching. The various schedules relate to what I take to be the deep pedagogical structures I referred to earlier. Supervisors using these schedules would discuss them with student teachers before teaching as part of the students' preparation and afterwards in a postactive evaluation. I discuss this process in more detail in a later chapter; at this stage, however, it might be useful if I devoted a little attention to the guide to problem solving to give an indication of the way I conceive this key skill and the rationale of the use of the schedules.

I should like to stress most earnestly that the schedule cannot be fully understood out of the full context of the argument in the book, and that if this brief consideration raises questions or doubts in readers' minds they should consult the original for elucidation. The context is, in fact, a detailed discussion of some important aspects of learning and instructional theory. The schedule assumes knowledge of this context and acts as an *aide-mémoire* to teachers, a checklist, as it were, to remind them of things to take into consideration in their teaching. It also acts as a point of focus for supervisor and student teacher when planning specific pieces of teaching. It is fairly brief, but each item rests on an understanding of quite complex principles.

SCHEDULE FOR THE TEACHING AND EVALUATION OF PROBLEM SOLVING (STEPS)

A Preactive

1 Analyse the task to clarify the nature of the problem to be solved.
2 Ascertain that the pupils have the necessary prerequisite capabilities.

B Interactive

3 Explain the nature of the problem to the pupils.
4 Encourage the pupils to range widely in their approaches to solving the problem.
5 Remind pupils of properties of the elements of the problem that might be useful.
6 Encourage pupils to make an analysis of the problem.
7 Prompt the pupils judiciously without solving the problem for them.
8 Provide feedback at key points.
9 Encourage an independent approach to problem solving by explaining methods of tackling problems.

C Evaluation

10 Present pupils with new problems of the same general type.

I make no claim that the above list is definitive, but I believe it includes the important elements in approaching the teaching of problem solving. However, the validity of the claim is almost irrelevant. The vital point is that problem solving is seen as a key skill to be taught and here is an approach to teach teachers to teach problem solving. I happen to be fond of the schedule reproduced above, a poor thing but mine own. But supervisors are not constrained by it. They are at liberty to modify or reject and still accept the view that problem solving is an important pedagogical skill that should be taught to all students, and that in itself is a very important commitment.

As I suggested above, the schedule is merely a very bald reminder of what has to be done. Each item is a simple rubric for some very complex matters. The first one, for example, refers to task analysis, in this case of the pupils' task in solving the problem. To teach problem solving effectively teachers need to be quite clear themselves what is involved. Not raised in the schedule, however, is the fact that teachers also have problems to solve: how best to tackle particular but varied teaching tasks.

Teaching concepts

Concept teaching is almost certainly the most ubiquitous teaching problem faced by teachers. It is also probably not very successfully accomplished if we are to believe recent reports and the general drift of the literature (Arnold 1981, DES 1981, DES 1982). Teaching concepts involves teaching facts, principles and generalizations in various fields of knowledge and the great problem, as I have mentioned earlier, is that all too often teachers teach the words that symbolize the concepts and not the concepts themselves.

I believe concept teaching is a key teaching skill and would classify it along with teaching problem solving as part of the deep structure of pedagogy that should support all teaching. In fact it contributes to successful problem solving. Without an understanding of the substance of a given field of study it is unlikely that a person will be able to solve problems in that field. Readers are referred to the original source (Stones 1979) for details of the argument about the teaching of concepts and the relevant schedule. Some of the items on the schedule are specific to the teaching of concepts and some are general and essential to other key teaching skills. Thus, for example, item nine in the *Schedule for the teaching of concepts* (*STOC*) suggests an activity specific to concept teaching: 'Provide new exemplars and non-exemplars and ask the pupils to identify the exemplars. Provide feedback for each discrimination.' Item one, on the other hand, is very general and has already featured in the problem-solving schedule: 'Make a task analysis of the teaching objectives to identify the key concepts involved, the subordinate concepts, specific examples, methods of presentation, pupils' activities and modes of evaluation.'

The teaching of motor skills and teaching for enhancing pupil motivation are two further key teaching skills proposed and discussed in detail in Stones 1979. As with the skills of problem solving and concept teaching they have their own specific aspects which are referred to in schedules related to the teaching and also include the more general skills that cut across all the specific ones.

Perhaps the key one of these general skills is that of task analysis, and I discuss this at length in the general discussion of pedagogy in Stones 1979. As I suggested earlier, the simple reminder to do a task analysis covers an enormously complex and difficult operation that student teachers need help and practice in. It demands an acquaintance with theoretical principles that cannot be derived by watching other teachers teach, and so a commitment to task analysis is a commitment to unifying practical teaching with a knowledge of theory. The same can be said about the other general items. Ascertaining the baseline competence of pupils and the quality of their learning at the end of instruction demands a far from superficial knowledge of the principles of evaluating learning. Both of these skills are, in my view, an absolutely crucial part of the basic pedagogic foundations of any teaching, no matter how individual teachers implement them in their own activity. Neither gets much attention at present in British training institutions.

Learning theory: learning 'theory'

Just as pupils are unlikely to solve problems if they have no knowledge of the field in which they are to solve them, so student teachers are unlikely to solve pedagogical problems if they have no understanding of key aspects of the way people learn. Thus the teaching schedules discussed above all have items that refer directly to aspects of learning theory. As with task analysis these items are common to all the schedules, with some slight differences. For example, the importance of feedback for learning, and methods of providing it to learners, are general and central concerns, which, once grasped by teachers, will equip them to meet completely new teaching situations with every chance of successfully arranging feedback to pupils. Similarly, an understanding of the role of reinforcement in pupils' learning, motivation and general affective states pervades all teaching actions and has profound implications for group interactions and classroom climate. The sad thing is that teachers are frequently not equipped by their training to distinguish between reinforcement and feedback, even less to take into account their effects in their teaching.

But pedagogical tasks are two edged: in addition to demanding an understanding of principles relating to teaching and learning they demand a grasp of the key generalizations in the subject field of study. This is so patently obvious that knowledge of the teaching subject has been taken by many people as sufficient for successful teaching instead of only being a necessary element in it. And this view has been in no small measure a cause of the past neglect of systematic pedagogy.

This neglect has been detrimental to the understanding by teachers of their field of study as well as of their teaching. I have found it a common experience with graduate student teachers and practising teachers alike that the process of carrying out a pedagogical analysis of the substantive content of their teaching has produced insights into the structure of key generalizations in the subject field that they did not possess before. Further, not infrequently, looking at bodies of principles in subject areas in the light of the type of analysis I have discussed above leads to a reappraisal of some commonly held views about the structure of knowledge in those areas. In some cases highly qualified and experienced people have come to the conclusion that their views on the nature of the knowledge in aspects of their specialist fields have been erroneous.

Skills and co-operative supervision

I suggest that the symbiotic nature of specialist subject knowledge and pedagogical theory has profound implications for supervision and the staffing of teacher training institutions. Equipping student teachers with basic teaching skills demands the study of theory and practice in both fields. This cannot be done in compartmentalized courses that separate subject knowledge from pedagogical knowledge and either or both from practical application. I hasten to say that this is not an advocacy of a return to 'mother hen' approaches to teacher training, but an argument for a challenging co-operative approach to the solution of practical teaching problems that involves high-level cognitive activity on the part of tutors specializing in different disciplines.

I make no suggestions as to whether the co-operation among tutors should be manifest in some form of group supervision, or whether some one person should act as co-ordinator, drawing appropriately on the expertise of colleagues. Given the varied nature of course provision in different institutions this is a matter in need of investigation. I am not unaware, however, that many institutions already operate systems that resemble the co-operative approach referred to. But I suggest that there is a considerable difference between a system in which persons designated as supervisors refer students to subject matter specialists, or occasionally 'education' special-ists for *ad hoc* consultancy on specific issues, and an approach that systematically and explicitly takes a co-operative multi-disciplinary focus on teaching students to solve pedagogical problems.

In Britain, in recent years, administrative pressures have operated contrary to this approach. The emphasis on the one-year course of training, following graduation in a specialist subject, has increased the proportion of student teachers following a course in which they are attached in the main to a tutor specialist in their subjects with some input from 'education' staff. The trend has been exacerbated by government emphases on specialist subjects and the complete ignoring of pedagogy. Nevertheless, I believe that the possibility of new approaches does exist and they could well develop, despite current pedagogical philistinism.

There is an obvious problem implicit in much of what I have been discussing that cannot and should not be avoided. It is that, given the present institutional course and administrative structures, the nature of recruitment to staff of training institutions, and the current expectations of tutor and super-visor roles, there is likely to be a need for staff development if anything like the approach to skill training discussed above is to be adopted. (Britain is not unique, however. The same point is taken in the report to the US Department of Education on *Design for a School of Pedagogy* (Smith 1980) which depicts a similar situation: the generally low level of pedagogical understanding in US teacher training institutions.) Paradoxi-cally, it seems to me, the expansion of postgraduate courses in teacher training may lead to a burgeoning of interest in pedagogy because subject specialists are genuinely concerned that their students teach their subjects effectively. Thus, when they encounter a discipline that offers hope of assisting them in achieving their aim, they are likely to feel positively towards it. Evidence of this was given at the conference on pedagogy mounted by the Committee for Research into Teacher Education in 1981, for example, by Merrick, the teaching of geography, Evans, the teaching of music, and Erskine, the teaching of painting. These subject specialists in training institutions had made a personal study of pedagogy in theory and practice that equipped them to marry the roles of subject specialist, pedagogical mentor and practical teaching supervisor.

This may not be the best method of operating, but it represented a very significant step forward for the tutors involved. I do not wish to suggest, however, that the future lies entirely with the subject specialists. Evans (1983), writing from the standpoint of a person with a main concern in the disciplines of education, describes how the adoption of a programme of teacher training based on the approach discussed above found that it helped students and tutors to solve some intransigent problems of course development in the B.Ed.(Hons) degree. In fact the message coming especially from the Evans study, but from others too, is that a pedagogical focus can act as a unifying element in the work of people in different subject specialisms and different aspects of educational studies. I discuss this question in greater detail later.

Teaching skills: a perspective

I have argued in this chapter that training student teachers in pedagogical skills is one of the most important responsibilities of supervisors. I have suggested that the skills to be nurtured are those that are general and fundamental to the teaching of *any* subject. I have also suggested that skills currently focused on are frequently *not* criterial to pupil learning although supervisors often devote considerable attention to them while neglecting the skills that are genuinely criterial. I should now like to discuss an approach to conceptualizing pedagogical skills that I believe helps supervisors to focus on the essential features of skill training and to identify skills genuinely criterial to pupil learning. I also suggest that it helps to ensure that the skills are not *ad hoc* unconnected agglomerations of atomistic activities but a matrix of interlocking actions based on coherent theoretical premises drawn from the study of human learning.

The essence of the approach is discussed in detail in Stones and Anderson (1972) and Stones (1979). It sees the important objectives of teaching as falling into three interdependent categories, each of which is relatable to general teaching skills. The basic type of learning in this categorization is the learning of concepts and principles in the field of pedagogy and other necessary subject studies, which, for convenience of reference, I refer to as type C learning. This type of learning is the bedrock of other kinds, which I discuss in more detail below. The other two, A and B, involve more complex activity by learners. It is probably appropriate here to make the point that I am not suggesting that the three categories embrace the total field of human learning, and I might illustrate this by referring to another type of learning that is commonly found in schools and out, the rote verbal learning that I have referred to earlier. I do not suggest that this is not of value in certain circumstances in school learning, merely that its use is limited. Concept learning is what most teachers try to encourage, and the point I made earlier was that rote learning was in default of concept learning.

Concept learning may be satisfying in itself and much of school learning may well aim to teach no more than that. But very frequently concept teaching is intended to make possible other activities. For example, learning bodies of concepts in the field of pedagogy may well be intrinsically interesting, but its main function is to enhance the efficacy of student teaching, and I suggest that competent practice by student teachers is the main aim of studying pedagogical theory. Another category of learning is a useful mediator between competent teaching and the learning of pedagogical concepts. It is acquiring the ability to appraise an example of teaching in the light of learned pedagogical concepts. This type of learning has something in common with the higher levels of the Bloom (1956) taxonomy of cognitive skills, and the skill of appraisal and evaluation developed resembles that involved in the use of protocol material (Smith 1969) which I discuss in greater detail later.

For ease of reference I refer to the skill of *carrying out* some form of activity in the light of theoretical principles, which I take to be a very complex activity, as a type A skill. The skill of *appraising* an activity in the light of those principles I refer to as a type B skill. The skill of demonstrating a grasp of the concepts that underpin type A and B skills I refer to as a type C skill. I stress that this skill must not be confused with rote verbal learning, and that it can only be identified by stringent methods of testing for concept learning and not merely rote verbalizing. Although for convenience it is useful to talk about the skills in terms of a hierarchy of complexity, it is misleading and, of course, arbitrary and hypothetical. However, I do believe it is useful and affords a conceptualization that is relatable to practical action and testable against it. But I stress that the skills are not related linearly but interpenetrate and are mutually refining, so that the complexity of learned concepts is increased through experience of attempting to apply them in the real world, and the elegance of practical activity is enhanced by the increased sophistication of the concept learning.

Table 4.1   The relationship between general skills and phases of teaching

Type of skill	Phases of teaching		
	Preactive	*Interactive*	*Evaluative*
A	Analyses task. Ascertains pupils' entry competence.	Teaches employing psychopedagogical principles.	Evaluates pupils' learning.
B	Evaluates an example of task analysis and pupil entry competence.	Evaluates an example of teaching in the light of psychopedagogical principles.	Evaluates an example of the assessment of childrens' learning.
C	Explains how the principles of task analysis and the ascertainment of entry competence apply to a specific teaching task.	Explains how the principles of psychopedagogy may be applied to a specific teaching task.	Explains how the principles of assessing pupils' learning may be applied to a specific teaching task.

Source: Stones, 1979, p.198.

To illustrate the proposed view of the interrelationship of the various skills I reproduce above a table from Stones (1979) which gives an example for three stages of a piece of teaching. The skill referred to at the interactive stage is perhaps rather bland since it does not refer to a particular aspect of pedagogical skills, but I hope the nature of the suggested relationship is clear.

As I have warned before in respect of other references to the source *Psychology of Education: A Pedagogical Approach*, the headings in the matrix relate to a detailed exposition of their constituent elements. In the case of the interactive section, for example, there is extended discussion of ways in which different aspects of learning theory may be drawn on to facilitate pupil learning of several different types such as I have discussed above: for example, concept learning, motor skill learning, problem solving. Similarly the other rubrics subsume approaches to the systematic application of ideas about generating objectives, carrying out task analysis and evaluating learning.

The two-way relationship of the skills suggests a guide to supervisor and student teacher action. It is useful to start at the bottom left and work upward and sideways to orient one to a logical method of proceeding. The upward progression alerts one to a logical and psychological relationship while the lateral movement takes account of the temporal progression in the actual teaching. However, throughout, it seems important to bear in mind that there is constant interaction among the different elements, that is, the main categories given in the matrix and the subcategories that constitute them. Thus, although we are taking an *analytical* approach, we are not taking an *atomistic* approach since we never lose sight of the total interrelationship. In practical terms of supervisor/student interaction, the approach assumes an early consideration of theoretical matters (bottom left) but sees this in close interaction with the other elements, so that adjacent elements interpenetrate closely.

I suggest that this type of approach is of considerable importance in introducing student teachers to elements of teaching skills. Without some form of pedagogical structure in the acquisition of teaching skills there is a serious danger of student teachers acquiring fragmented collections of heterogeneous activities, drawn from conventional wisdom encapsulated in traditional supervisor checklists, or set out in guides to specific skills in microteaching. There is also a need to take an approach to supervision that avoids this fragmentation and provides a framework for supervisor action. I make some proposals towards an approach of this nature in a later chapter.

5

. . . .

Pedagogy of supervision

The logic of the discussion so far leads to a conception of supervision as a form of teaching: and, I suggest, if consistent, to a commitment by supervisors to the same pedagogy as that they seek to teach their students. Thus the discussion of some of the key teaching skills in the previous chapter relates importantly to supervisors' own activities. In fact it is reasonable to take the view alluded to earlier, of supervision as being one of a universe of specific exemplifications of teaching in general. Each specific exemplification has its own idiosyncratic elements that distinguish it from others, but all are embraced by the same general pedagogical principles. It should, therefore, be possible for supervisors in the process of helping students to learn to teach to discuss their, the supervisors', own procedures to illuminate the procedures the students are striving to grasp.

If this all seems rather complex or convoluted I suggest it is because we are discussing a very complex phenomenon. Life is much easier if one takes a transmission view of teaching and just tells the student teachers how to tell the pupils. But if one takes the view of teaching and supervision proposed in earlier discussions one enters the Chinese box world I mentioned previously, where talk about teaching is nested within similar talk about supervising and one needs to keep a firm grip in discussion to avoid slipping from one to the other without noticing. It gets even more complicated when one talks about teaching and learning to supervise as I do in later chapters. Nevertheless, the fact that all the talk relates to pervasive general principles of teaching, but in varying manifestations, enriches the discourse of all participants.

The degree of enrichment naturally depends on the depth of understanding of the principles by the participants in the discourse. If tutors do, in fact, employ didactic transmission methods in retailing their views of principles of learning, it is unlikely that the discourse will be very stimulating. And the reason for this is to be found in the very principles of learning that should form the basis for discussion.

This point can be illustrated by reference to one of the basic skills discussed in the previous chapter: that is, teaching for concept learning. I tried to make the point there that if teachers try to teach concepts by transmission methods, i.e. telling the pupils, the pupils are likely to learn little, if anything, more than the words themselves. By the same token, merely telling student teachers about the principles of learning could well have the same effect, so that engaging students in discussion demanding deep understanding of those principles would be very unlikely to prove profitable. For it to be otherwise supervisors have no alternative but to practise what they preach, that is, adopt a structured approach to teaching the principles they see as relevant to the successful teaching of concepts making use of the same principles. That approach will demand methods other than transmission methods.

Supervisors practising what they preach will be able to enrich their teaching in a most unusual way. If they make their pedagogy explicit to their students they will not only signal to them that the principles informing supervisors' teaching have real practical application, but they will enlarge the field of tutorial discourse so as to include their own teaching. Undoubtedly some supervisors will find this prospect unattractive and threatening, but it need not be so, and there is little doubt that the consideration of the supervisors' teaching as well as the students' provides that variety of exemplification so crucial for the learning of general principles. One other very important aspect of this approach is its value to supervisors who are in a position to get informed feedback about their own teaching so that the supervisor/student interaction is a genuine learning experience for both.

Learning theory and teaching concepts

Adopting the exploratory and co-operative approach to teaching I have advocated precludes one using transmission methods of teaching; adopting the pedagogy suggested provides guidance for the implementation of the approach. In particular, having as a main focus the objective of helping student teachers to acquire skills to enable them to solve a wide variety of teaching problems, provides an orientation towards identifying important supervisory activities.

This focus is the one proposed in the discussion of the objectives of supervision. In that discussion I suggested an approach to identifying objectives that took the overall objective and attempted to analyse it into subordinate objectives whose achievement would contribute to the achievement of the main objective. This method of proceeding helps to reveal the inner nature of the teaching problem and thereby shed light on possible effective teaching strategies. An approach to the analysis of the actual teaching task, such as suggested earlier, adds a different dimension and helps to pinpoint more precisely specific teaching activities. Since we are currently considering supervision as a specific exemplification of teaching we may take the general approach as a heuristic guide to arriving at our hoped-for destination of producing independent and effective pedagogical problem solvers.

It is inconceivable that a person could solve pedagogical problems without some knowledge of how people learn. It is therefore incumbent on staff of training institutions to introduce students to the subject. The traditional approach through lectures, reading, seminars and the like has been questioned earlier, not necessarily because of the teaching *method* which has often been the subject of 'research' (lectures versus reading, etc.) but because of the nature of their underlying pedagogy and because of the separation between courses purveying the theory and the activity of student teaching. I now consider some possible ways of overcoming the pedagogical problems of teaching the 'theory' of teaching.

I suggest it is productive when talking about 'theory' in teaching that we have in mind those concepts from the educational disciplines that seem to us to be of value in enhancing pupil learning of all types. The task of supervisors is so to arrange students' learning experiences that they acquire those concepts and not just the words. The supervisory task, then, is teaching how to teach concepts, and if there is any validity in the theoretical principles being taught then they must of necessity be employed by supervisors themselves. It is at this juncture that the conflict between apprenticeship modes of learning to teach and theory-based modes becomes apparent.

One of the prime tenets of concept learning is that one cannot learn concepts by encountering solely non-exemplars. Another element is that one needs feedback to confirm or disconfirm one's suppositions or hypotheses about the nature of the phemonena one is currently attempting to categorize. There are other important aspects to concept learning but for the moment let us consider supervision in the light of these two.

In a way they are intertwined. Consider the exemplars of teaching which all who have been through formal schooling have experienced. It is my view that for most of us there will have been a heavy loading of non-exemplars of concept teaching. In the current apprenticeship mode of learning teaching, when student teachers go into schools, in general they continue the same process of random exposure to exemplars of teaching they have experienced as pupils. Many of these exemplars will be negative as far as concept teaching is concerned. But the chances are very high that the students will not know whether or not they have ever experienced a teacher arranging learning experiences so as to optimize concept learning, because no one will have ever given them feedback *vis à vis* any hypotheses they may have on the subject. Indeed, if they experience mostly transmission teaching, with an accent on rote learning, their ideas of good teaching may well be limited to that approach to teaching and their eyes will be closed to other methods. Supervisors may thus be faced with the difficult problem of trying to break into a closed circle with very powerful, if unconscious and unsuspected, peripheral defences if they endeavour to teach students how to teach concepts.

Concept teaching and supervision

I have made some suggestions about tackling the problem of teaching for conceptual learning (Stones 1979, pp.196–226), and I suggest that most of the elements in the heuristic proposed there are amenable to application to supervision seen as teaching. Supervisors following an approach of this nature will attempt to breach the closed circle of imitative learning by drawing students' attention to the findings of work in the field of human learning. In the schedule I propose as a heuristic for concept learning generally (Stones 1979, pp.205–6), I draw attention to the need to provide for the programmed provision of exemplars of the concepts being taught to ensure meaningful learning.

In terms of supervisory activity this implies providing a carefully chosen and sequenced series of exemplars to illustrate to students the nature of the teaching under consideration. Verbal exposition will not do. The observation of actual teaching is a possible way of proceeding, but other aspects of the schedule suggest other and probably more useful ways of proceeding in the early stages of student learning. The point is that classroom transactions are so complex that neophytes would find it most difficult to identify those aspects of the activity that were the object of attention. The schedule applied to supervision would therefore suggest that supervisors help students to acquire concepts about concept teaching, or about problem solving, or reinforcement, by providing them with a graded series of exemplars in which the confusion of total classroom interactions is reduced greatly in the early stages of their learning and gradually built up to full classroom strength as the students become more competent.

It is not, however, just a matter of increasing the signal to noise ratio in the beginning and gradually reversing it later. It is also a question of judiciously introducing criterial attributes of the concept of how best to teach concepts, or problem solving, or motor skills, or reinforcement, in such a way that the complexity of the operation increases. The increase in complexity is likely to be because of the increasing number of criterial attributes but could also be a function of the complexity of the attributes themselves. The skill of the supervisor lies first in identifying the criterial attributes and then in arranging a programme to take the students from ignorance to understanding of the concepts relating to competent teaching. There is a world of difference between this approach and the current totally random exposure to kaleidoscopic classroom events. But it cannot be stressed too much that, although the graduated approach may seem to be keeping students away from the real world with which they have to come to terms with some day, they will eventually make much more sense of the complexities of classroom processes than if they were to be plunged straight into things. It is the difference between being thrown into the deep end and getting there by learning to swim from the shallow end.

Nor should it be forgotten that we are talking about presenting students with examples of teaching for their scrutiny, not just talking about processes in teaching. The examples may be looked upon as models of pared-down teaching encounters accentuating different aspects of teaching. They could be small demonstrations by the tutor or teachers. They could be video recordings or audio recordings or even transcripts of teaching episodes.

A method I have used is to concatenate, from examples of specific aspects of teaching on videotape, short samples illustrative of different criterial elements of important pedagogical concepts. For example, a series of short pieces of teaching illustrating reinforcement as practised by various teachers presents to students exemplars that vary as to subject, to teacher, to age of pupils, to physical conditions, all of which are non-criterial attributes of the use of reinforcing moves by the teachers. Similarly the modalities are varied: verbal/nonverbal, tangible/intangible (e.g. token reinforcement versus commendation), group/individual, teacher-pupil/pupil-pupil and so on. Here is a great variety of exemplifications of which the majority of the most salient aspects are non-criterial. The abiding criterial attributes remain the same although everything else changes. In this example the principle of the creation by teachers of a learning environment that will result in pupils' greater engagement in learning activities and continue their activity at strength over long periods is the key attribute. The means by which reinforcement is implemented is often a matter for individual ingenuity although, of course, there is a good deal of information about the reinforcing effects of teacher activities such as attending to pupils, or praising them, or arranging for the pupils to experience success in their activity, and these must all be brought to students' attention. Indeed, it may be thought by some that most of the last points are criterial, and especially one thinks of the experience of success. It would be a mistake, however, to think of any one phenomenon as criterial unless it is quite inconceivable to have reinforcement without it. If they are taken to be criterial and accepted by students as being so, difficulties could arise by students imagining that by praising pupils they would be reinforcing them when, in some circumstances, peer attitudes might be such as to dictate that teacher praise would be unwelcome and a punisher rather than a reinforcer.

In fact what I am suggesting is an approach to teaching students that lays emphasis on very general principles and cautions against the mechanical application of specific approaches to implementing the principles. At the same time I also consider that supervisors should introduce students to those teacher activities that have been shown to be of value in implementing the general principles. Thus, in the case of reinforcement, various examples of teacher praise, attention, nonverbal actions, careful structuring of learning experiences for pupil success are all essential to build up concepts of the nature of reinforcement and, at the same time, indicate to students means by which they may be able to arrange it successfully in their teaching.

I do not suggest in any way that the activities referred to above are to be solely supervisor directed. Although the tutor actions I have mentioned are all calculated to help students to understand in a meaningful way (that is, learn concepts about) the process of teaching for understanding and enjoyment, they can be greatly assisted by discussion with peers and tutors, and with teachers in the schools they visit. Nor should the pupils themselves be overlooked. They may have more to contribute than we currently imagine (Meighan 1977). In fact, discussions of this type in seminars or other groups help greatly to sharpen up the participants' understanding, always provided that they are genuine exchanges and not supervisor or tutor dominated, a form of small group transmission session.

Protocols and pedagogical skills

Readers will probably have made the connection between this discussion of the teaching of the concepts from learning theory that may be of use to student teachers and the proposed categorization of teaching objectives and skills discussed in the previous chapter. I said there that concept teaching is probably one of the most ubiquitous aims of teaching, all too often, unfortunately, in implementation, honoured more in the breach than in the observance. I suggested that the learning involved was not the highest to which teachers should aspire for themselves or their pupils but that it was an essential prerequisite for more complex types of learning. I categorized the teaching of concepts as a skill at a level I designated level C, in view of my suggestion that there were, in addition, two more complex general skills that built on concept learning.

The first type of skill that I suggest involves more complex activity than the learning of concepts is the utilization of learned concepts in appraisal and evaluation of phenomena related to the learned concepts. This type B activity applied to teaching demands that student teachers are skilled at appraising specimens of teaching in the light of principles they have learned about teaching, and of evaluating that teaching. That is, they would not just give an assessment of the teaching as being good, bad or indifferent, but would be able to evaluate the teaching being appraised in terms of the way it exemplified aspects of relevant theory from human learning. The argument for this type of activity in the progression of student teachers' learning is that it refines their understanding of the concepts they have been learning and prepares them for a self-critical approach to their own implementation of those principles in their own teaching.

Supervisors making use of this approach in their teaching will typically use real examples of teaching, or teaching recorded in some way via video, audio or printed media. There will be a crucial difference, however, both between the material they use and the use they make of it, and the use they made of models when they taught the concepts in the first place. The specimens of teaching are not models, they are protocols (Smith 1969). The difference is that protocols are often unedited material whereas models are carefully chosen and structured and, indeed, could well be staged. Protocols present teaching in all its complexity for students to analyse and appraise. Naturally they will do this in co-operation with the supervisor and preferably also with their peers. In fact, the role of the supervisor is still very important since, although protocols are slices of real life, the idea of the gradual increase in complexity and task difficulty is still very important and the supervisor's skill is manifested in the optimum gradient of complexity as the protocols are presented to students.

The exercise of appraising protocol material in the field of human learning and teaching is a taxing task. From the complexity of a variety of examples the students have to identify the basic common principles as they are exemplified in practical situations. The problem is compounded by the life experience of the student teachers and the stereotypical view of teaching that most of us carry around with us. That stereotype is likely to be one where there is one adult standing in front of a group of pupils and telling them something, whether the location is under an African tree, or a room at Eton, or at Greyfriars, or a Chinese commune school. Most of us would agree that the location is a non-criterial attribute of the concept of teaching, but what about the image of the adult confronting a group of children? Is this criterial? In other words, does it have to be like that? This is just one of the questions that the use of protocols presents very sharply. Whether or not a supervisor accepts my view that the expository mode is no more criterial to effective teaching than the locality does not affect the value of protocol material to elucidate the nature of the approach as it relates to theoretical notions. A supervisor who does take my view, however, may well have a more difficult job in counselling students about their teaching because of the much greater complexity of teaching situations. Focusing on the teaching task of getting pupils to learn with optimum effectiveness and then trying to work out the most useful way of carrying out the task will involve supervisors in selecting a variety of protocol material that may not be strictly representative of the pattern of teaching as it is now. This, it seems to me, is what supervisors should be doing unless one takes the view that their brief is to maintain the *status quo*.

The adoption of protocols, in group teaching sessions such as seminars, will normally involve the use of recorded material to form the basis for discussion where 'theory and reality meet' (Grant 1976). Grant quotes Gleisman (1972), who summarizes the argument behind the use of protocols as first put forward by B. O. Smith in the statement: 'For many years we have been concerned in teacher education with bridging the gap between theory and practice. . . . What we have not clearly understood, however, is that it is in the process of *interpreting behaviour in concrete situations* that theory and reality meet'. Grant describes the development and use of a protocol that draws on Piaget's theories relating to the development of schemas in learning. She used a self-instructional teaching programme (Stones 1968) to explain the ideas, and a video recording of a small group of parents discussing education with a teacher as protocol material that exemplified the development of a schema in a genuine learning situation. This example also bears on the point I made earlier about the possibilities of variation and atypicality in the selection of protocols.

There is a further, very important aspect to the use of protocols. It lays the foundation for the development of skills that are absolutely vital for teachers if they are to be capable of self critical appraisal and competent to take remedial action as a result of this appraisal. This is a theme to which I shall return in more detail later.

Pedagogical problem solving

The work of supervisors in the field of concept teaching and the use of protocols is a gradual progression towards the key skill: the ability by student teachers to identify, analyse and solve pedagogical problems in a variety of conditions. I referred to the prior learning in terms of C skills and B skills, and both are essential for theory-based teaching that offers the hope of informed and effective self-monitoring when students complete their training. The actual intervention of the supervisor into students' acquisition of the type A skill naturally demands that they actually engage in practice teaching, but there is more to it than their just going into a classroom to teach and the supervisors' guidance is important here. These remarks hark back to Table 4.1 which sets out a matrix of types of skill and phases of teaching. It reminds us about the importance of activities prior to teaching and after teaching, and the importance of supervisory guidance in the planning and evaluation phase. In the evaluation phase the use of recorded material is again of considerable value. This time the recording will be of students' own teaching so that they in effect reflect back upon their own work as they did on the protocols earlier.

In view of the complexity of this phase of supervision and teaching I devote a more comprehensive discussion to it later. However, before leaving the subject of the relation of teaching skills to supervision I should like to comment briefly on a possible conceptual difficulty arising from the Chinese box situation I discussed earlier. It relates to the place of other aspects of educational studies in the teaching of pedagogical skills. In other chapters I have referred to these studies and have, I hope, given some indication of my views on the subject. In this chapter, however, I am solely concerned with the way in which supervisors can draw on notions from learning theory to enhance their own effectiveness in helping student teachers to acquire concepts and skills related to teaching. It is entirely up to individual supervisors to make their own decisions about the concepts they think it important for their students to acquire, but to optimize students' learning they will probably find great advantage in taking the line suggested. For example, there is likely to be little argument that teachers need to take home background and the environment of the school into account, in their approach to teaching, and it follows that students should also take it into account, as should the training institution in its turn. This is a curriculum matter but the *substance* of the discussion in this chapter has been on the *process* of concept learning and its practical implementation in teaching and not on the *substantive* content of the concepts thought important for students to take into account in their teaching. I will return to this question in later chapters when we probe a little more deeply into the specifics of supervision.

6

· · · · · · · · · ·

Instrumentation in supervision

Schedules

In Britain in the late 1960s analytical approaches to the study of classroom processes were little known and, indeed, this gap in professional awareness was the main reason for the publication in the early 1970s of a book whose aim was to bring the work that was going on to the attention of British educationists working in the field of teacher preparation (Stones and Morris 1972b). The same global approach was to be found in the way in which supervisors approached their task. Whatever the nature of the advice given informally to students during the course of teaching practice, institutions by and large trafficked in generalities, so that student teacher assessment following practical teaching would as likely as not be of the nature of a 'pen portrait' commenting on the student's performance. An example of the genre might read: 'Miss X has largely followed the existing regime in the classroom and consequently her work has been less ambitious and imaginative than one would like . . . she has raised the standards of the children's writing . . . ' (Stones and Morris 1972a). The survey from which this example comes was conducted in 1970 and found that at that time few institutions used analytical rating scales. Since then there has undoubtedly been movement towards a more analytical approach to the appraisal of teaching by supervisors and a great increase in the use of schedules for assessment of teaching using analytical categories. (See McCulloch 1979.)

In view of the fact that Sidney Morris and I argued for the development of an analytical approach to the examination and appraisal of practical teaching, it would be churlish not to welcome this change. However I do not think the way things have gone is an unmixed blessing. 'Discovery' of the approach was followed by its fashionable adoption, and often the schedules were more impressive as to form than content. The undoubted benefit has been to explicate the perceived main aspects of criteria of teacher competence so that they can be scrutinized and discussed. However, some have embalmed the trivial and the cosmetic, and if these become narrowly specific and prescriptive on supervisors, the net effect could well be to produce a system worse than before. The types of problems attached to some of these schedules are twofold. On the one hand many of the items are ill defined categories that are at times vapid to the point of vacuousness. On the other hand many of the less vague ideas are mere encapsulations of conventional wisdom, checklists of tips for teachers with little or no relation to pedagogical theory or concern for children's learning, a question I have already discussed in earlier chapters.

Nevertheless there have been some very encouraging developments in the design of schedules that indicate a considerable advance in the last decade. An indication of these developments may be summed up in a preamble to the use of one of the guides in McCulloch's survey (p.101). 'The assessment of practical teaching involves the balancing of so many complex variables, many of them tacit, that it must necessarily be a matter for professional judgement of qualified persons.' The new development now needed is the enhancement of the professional judgement of those 'qualified persons'.

It may be that the present generation of schedules represents an unavoidable stage of development. Until they began to appear it was not possible to make any movement towards real agreement about desirable criterial attributes of good teaching. As long as methods of adjudication comprised global statements such as *good* or *bad* with no elucidation, the best that could be hoped for was imprecise agreement on the subject of competent teaching or, more likely, a spurious consensus.

With the items spelled out as they are now in many schedules the way is open for debate and discussion about their nature, and this should enable teacher educators and particularly supervisors to make progress towards devising instruments that can be of more genuine pedagogical value to student teachers than many are at the present.

Types of instruments

BLUNT

Although I have talked about 'schedules' so far as though they were all of a piece, in fact they are infinitely varied, if only in particulars, as though the followers of fashion adopted a common general style but added idiosyncratic touches to assert their independence and personal taste. Nevertheless, although it may not be strictly true to say that when you have seen one you have seen them all, the type of instruments used in British teacher education for assessment of teaching are much of a muchness. In the main they are home-grown versions of the genre of the *Stanford Teacher Competence Appraisal Guide* which was developed in the late 1950s and early 1960s. It is indicative of the spread of these instruments that most people now in British teacher education institutions will have seen a copy of this guide whereas it had hardly been heard of in the early 1970s. Students of the history of education, however, and especially the afficionados of school log books, may well have a sense of *déjà vu* as they contemplate the categories in the *STCAG*, a point that I made earlier when I gave an example of an item from a schedule used by a schools inspector about hundred years ago.

SHARPER

The salient common attribute of the instruments just discussed is probably the attempt they make to take a more detailed look at the overall performance of the teacher in the classroom, and in some cases, including the *STCAG*, the scrutiny extends beyond the classroom. Other schedules have been developed with a finer focus on teacher activities, especially in conjunction with microteaching and the practice by student teachers of specific teaching skills. Schedules of this type have typically followed the examples set in the early work on microteaching at Stanford in identifying a smaller number of teacher activities relating to what the authors considered to be key teaching skills (Allen and Ryan 1969, Brown 1975).

An example of these schedules that may be taken as illustrative of the genre lists four specific teacher activities in connection with the teacher's use of reinforcement. The type of things referred to are whether and how much the teacher used verbal reinforcers such as 'Good', 'Fine', etc., what nonverbal encouragers the teacher used, and the teacher's accepting pupils' responses even if they were not fully correct. Four items cover these points but in both the Allen and Ryan and the Brown expositions the schedule is contextualized in a discussion about the nature of the activity.

Other schedules that may be found in the literature on microteaching include such things as beginning a lesson, closure, i.e. drawing the lesson or part of the lesson to a satisfactory conclusion, the use of different types of question, teacher liveliness, pupil participation in the lesson and teaching for concept formation. This is by no means an exhaustive list but it does impart a flavour of the type of thing one might encounter under the rubric of microteaching skill schedules. However, the point I made about the variety in the more global schedules also applies to these more specific ones. For the most part these schedules are unpublished institutional products that all tend to owe something to the early Stanford model, although expressed in their own particular ways which might range from a fairly bald statement of just a few points to be watched to a reasoned statement and explanation of the rationale for the instrument. The latter type was used in the early 1970s in the University of Stirling microteaching programme and, more than most, relates to theoretical principles derived from studies of human learning and comprises a much more unitary collection of schedules than many. There is no denying, however, that in the main there is a lack of conceptual coherence among the catalogue of skills.

This lack of conceptual coherence among the schedules is most likely the outcome of the mongrel nature of their progenitures. The main ancestral lines seem to be ideas from some aspects of psychology, and to some extent from conventional classroom wisdom, although the latter is not as much in evidence as it is in the more general schedules. However, the way in which these more specific schedules have been used has, in general, probably been more productive than have the global ones. One important contribution from this field was the idea of a re-teach. This procedure involved the student teacher in a dialogue with the supervisor after teaching a lesson, with the aim of identifying strengths and weaknesses in the teaching. This counselling was to be a guide to the student so that the lesson could be taught again with a comparable group of pupils in the hope of expectation that there would be an improvement in performance.

Although in many cases the idea of the re-teach was dropped, usually for administrative rather than pedagogical reasons, it was an important injection into thinking about supervision. Whereas the notion behind the use of general schedules was usually in the assessment of teaching performance for ultimate certification, microteaching schedules were clearly for formative rather than summative evaluation. This was an important development because it shifted the emphasis of supervision from assessment to guidance.

The supervisor in microteaching plays a more active part in student training than happens in traditional methods of school visiting. Although in many cases of traditional supervision the teaching practice is prepared for and lessons discussed with the supervisor, there is not likely to be the same degree of prior consultation contingent upon the employment of the more specific schedules. The use of schedules related to specific skills leads to the instrument itself changing the nature of the operation by making different demands on students and staff whose role expectations change and in turn modify the skills appropriate to supervisions.

It should be noted that it is the use of the schedule that effects the change in the supervisor/student relationship, and not the fact that the teaching is usually video recorded. It is perfectly possible to video record teaching and carry on more or less as usual as far as the follow-up session goes. That is, the supervisory dialogue could be conducted in terms of the commonly observed generalities of supervision. Of course, the recording provides a powerful aid in the counselling and naturally modifies the nature of the discourse, but so long as the discourse remains within the common categories of conventional supervision the change is not fundamental. The survey by Fuller and Manning (1973) bears on this point.

Life in classrooms

Other recent developments that have significant implications for supervision are connected with the study of life in classrooms. A variety of disciplines has become very interested in the taken-for-granted but highly intriguing social grouping of one adult and a number of younger people involved in a relationship whose nature is variously and not too clearly understood. Among those interested, whose probings are relevant to the concerns of supervisors, are sociologists, social psychologists and psycholinguists. Their investigations have not been pedagogic in intent but have alerted us to nuances of social interactions that cannot be ignored in any study of teaching or attempts to improve it.

Not all studies of classroom life have involved the use of instrumentation. In fact, some workers have done their best to avoid imposing any sort of structure on their observations by adopting 'fly on the wall' tactics and making records of classroom events as they happen, frequently using imaginative recording techniques such as time-lapse photography (e.g. Walker and Adelman 1975). Others have been sceptical about the possibility of really 'telling it like it is', arguing that if you go into the classroom to record what goes on without a checklist in your hand, you almost certainly have one in your head even though you may not be fully aware of the fact. Of the approaches that have consistently used forms of instruments to record classroom events probably the most influential contribution has come from various studies of verbal interaction. Bales (1950) was one of the first to use this approach to the analysis of group processes and this was developed and applied to classrooms, especially in the work of Flanders (1970), but followed up in the work of countless other investigators. The proliferation of category systems has been a spectacular example of the phenomenon referred to in the discussion about the creation of various forms of global assessment schedules for student teaching. Simon and Boyer (1974) in America and Galton (1978) in Britain have produced catalogues of these instruments which now run into the hundreds. Supervisors can make use of these instruments in their discussions with students, not only to draw their attention to the complexities and significance of classroom discourse, but also as possible tools to use in discussing students' teaching with them in the supervisory interview.

Heuristic guides

The instruments so far discussed have mainly been *post hoc* as far as student teaching and supervision are concerned. Mainly, but not entirely, as my comments on the use of schedules in microteaching indicate. They have also tended to be *ad hoc* so that the combined effect is like the one described above that lacks conceptual unity and accentuates the evaluative aspect of supervision rather than the supportive/helping aspect. I have suggested that some approaches to microteaching have the potential for changing the nature of supervision towards the supportive/helping aspect. I now suggest that the incipient tendency needs to be made explicit prior to practice, and firmly rooted in a body of theoretical pedagogical principles that forms the substance of the students' professional studies and from which their practice may draw sustenance.

I have attempted to form a basis for a supervisor/student relationship of this type by the development of the schedules referred to in chapter four. As I indicated there, the rationale of these schedules is to provide encapsulations in the form of guides to practical activity of key aspects of theory that seem to hold promise for the enhancement of student teaching and pupil learning. Unlike many other schedules, these instruments are not comprehensible outside the context of theoretical discussion such as that provided in the body of the book in which they are published. The argument in the book is not just an extended gloss on the schedules. The schedules and the argument are closely interwoven. However, the point is made in the book that the argument can be tested only in practice. By the same token, the use of these instruments by supervisors is only possible by changing the nature of supervision along the lines I suggest. Instruments of this type act as interfaces between theory and practice and as prosthetic devices (La Barre 1954), adding to the power of supervisors and also calling forth new skills *in the supervisor*.

The schedules themselves comprise an attempt to provide a checklist of key teacher activities that are likely to enhance pupil learning, based on the exposition of principles enunciated in the text. They adopt the approach discussed in the chapter on objectives. One schedule, the *Schedule for the Evaluation of Teaching* (*SET*) consists of twelve items intended to remind teachers of a broad sweep of teacher activities. Four more specific schedules form a second level in a hierarchy. They are: *Schedule for the Teaching of Concepts* (*STOC*), *Schedule for the Teaching of Evaluation of Problem Solving* (*STEPS*), *Schedule for the Teacher's Use of Reinforcement* (*STUR*), and *Schedule for the Teaching of Psychomotor Skills* (*STOPS*). Each of the items on the schedules can be broken down still further and form the basis of discussion between supervisor and student and a guide to student activity. Some items run through all the schedules and there is no suggestion at all of compartmentalization. The analytical approach is adopted to break down large teaching problems into smaller ones in a rational and reasonable psychological manner and not to suggest that the teacher pay attention to only one thing at a time.

Since the schedules provide two levels of generality (*SET* subsumes the others), and since each schedule has a number of specific items that could merit attention in their own right, supervisors and students using the schedules are in a position to put specific examples of teaching through filters of increasing fineness. Examples could be models used at the earlier part of the teaching phase of supervision or protocols at a later stage. But possibly most potent of all, the schedules could provide guides for the discussion of students' own teaching using video recordings as protocol material. Whatever approach is adopted, supervisor and student will decide on the most appropriate way of proceeding through the hierarchy at any one time. Thus on some occasions the general schedule, *SET*, might be a useful point of departure, while on other occasions it might be preferable to start with one of the more specific instruments. In the early stages of supervision when the supervisor is introducing the student to elements of teaching theory, it may well be most appropriate to focus on specific items on the schedules to provide a focus for the development by the student of bodies of pedagogical principles.

Clearly the object of this progressive filtering is diagnostic and ameliorative. It therefore bespeaks a long-term student/ supervisor relationship in which both parties are involved in the identification and implementation of teaching strategies and tactics informed by theory. Single-shot supervision, such as is often practised at the moment where the supervisor meets the student for the first time on teaching practice, is of doubtful value and can achieve little. The mutual engagement by student and supervisor in attempts to solve pedagogical problems radically changes the nature of supervision, and the instruments are guides to action not attempts to measure student competence *post hoc*.

Schedules: grading or guiding?

Schedules used by supervisors currently are, in fact, more likely than not to be used to assess student teaching competence primarily rather than for the systematic guidance of student learning. I have discussed this usage in earlier chapters and have drawn attention to some of the difficulties attached to it. However, the relationship between attitudes towards assessment and the use of schedules is one that demands careful attention. I say this because of the preoccupation with the grading of students to be found in some institutions of higher education in Britain, and the touching faith of their staff in their ability to make fine distinctions between different people's competence as teachers. The combination of the two attitudes impedes the development of approaches to supervision that stress development and de-emphasize assessment.

Current custom is for schedules for the assessment of teaching practice to comprise a set of categories that are rated on a scale ranging from poor to good or excellent. For example, the Stanford Guide has items such as *Clarity of aims*, *Organization of the lesson*, and *Clarity of presentation*. These are graded on a seven-point scale from 'weak' to 'truly exceptional' with a category 'unable to observe'. This example may be taken as reasonably typical of British practice. Some examples culled from McCulloch's (1979) survey read: *Speech and general behaviour*, *Concern for truth* and *Classroom organization and management*. These are also graded along similar scales with the five-point scale probably the favourite.

The presuppositions upon which the ratings of the various items are based and the way the ratings are used are important and difficult issues for supervisors. Supervisors using these scales within traditional norm-reference conventions will be oriented towards producing a predetermined spread of marks, probably approximating roughly to the Gaussian curve. The post-assessment treatment of the marks is the next crucial question. In some institutions some form of aggregation may be used to arrive at a global rating, in others the ratings on the items will be taken to provide a 'profile' of the student's competence and no global mark will be reported. However, pressures to provide final global gradings for determining degree class are hard to resist and many training institutions resort to psychometrically indefensible practices such as combing raw scores from different instruments to achieve that end.

But whether or not scores are aggregated, the crucial feature of the norm-referenced approach is that ratings are based on comparing one person's performance with another's. The question in the rater's mind will be of the nature: 'Is this teacher below average, above average or average on this particular item?' This approach in itself begs many questions, some of which I have discussed earlier. Even assuming that an item is validly related to good teaching, which itself demands an enormous suspension of disbelief, other difficulties remain. Given the complexity of teaching, of individual differences among teachers, of differences among and within groups of pupils, and the fact that every teaching situation is unique, making distinctions among teachers means comparing very different things. It is not only far more difficult than is generally considered but also, since it implicitly posits an ideal performer, it has an inbuilt mechanism to reward conformity to the ideal image. Supervisors, being human, are likely to favour those who conform to their image, a point discussed earlier.

It is possible to conceive of another approach to the question of grading the items on schedules. This procedure makes no attempt to compare teachers, de-emphasizes or eschews assessment, and instead emphasizes guidance of student teacher action diagnostically to provide ameliorative feedback towards the refinement of teaching skills. The approach is akin to that of criterion-referenced testing in which learning is evaluated according to the extent to which it approximates to predetermined levels of competence. Easier said than done. Difficult enough in apparently simple tests of pupil learning; in the case of student teacher learning of teaching skills it is dauntingly complex.

In using the schedules for the development of pedagogical skills that I referred to earlier, I have adopted a method of rating the items that attempts to avoid comparing people and instead takes a criterion-referenced approach. This is very difficult in view of the complexity of the behaviour involved, and there is a great tendency for normative influences to intrude. However, the fact that the items are explicitly related to theoretical premises on the one hand and to the accomplishment of pupil learning on the other gives supervisors and students a better purchase on the problem than is the case with differently derived schedules. The task is made much more tractable and effective by the use of video recordings, and I believe these are of great importance in developing a rigorous system of supervision. I return to this question later; the point I wish to develop here relates to their value in arriving at some degree of 'objectivity' in rating the items on the pedagogical schedules.

Recordings make it possible to view a piece of teaching with several things in mind, and to cope with them all in a way that would be quite impossible without them. Using the pedagogy schedules with recordings one is able to focus on one or a small selection of teacher behaviours at a time and rerun the tape to view other activities later. Basing their evaluation of the recorded activity on their understanding of pedagogical theory, supervisor and student are able to arrive at an appraisal of what the student teacher *did* as compared with what he or she *should have done* in the light of the relevant pedagogical principles and the actual conditions existing at the time in the classroom. This technique, I suggest, puts the rating of the schedule items on a similar footing to scoring in criterion-referenced testing.

I believe that this approach avoids the problems of assessment by adjudicating among people. I also believe that the diagnostic use of the instrument introduces a new element into supervision and the appraisal of student teaching. Since the different items in the schedule relate to different important facets of teaching for particular purposes, the careful appraisal of students' scores on the individual items, looked at together, makes up pictures of their teaching that provide information not about how they compare with others, but about the nature of their expertise in different aspects of teaching for different purposes. That is, the students obtain a profile of their *current* style of teaching. This profile says no more than that on item A of the schedule a particular student performs more competently than on item B.

The profile obtained in this way resembles an ipsative scale such as the Allport-Vernon-Lindzey scale of values (1960). The difference is, however, that the scale obtained from the pedagogical schedules approximates to criterion referencing, whereas the scale of values is norm referenced in that it tells individuals the extent to which they deviate from norms derived from various populations. The profiles developed from both, however, may be looked at similarly. In the scale of values the point is to reveal to individuals whether, for example, their interest or commitment to a religious set of values is greater or less than their interest and commitment to economic or social values as measured by the generalized sets of values held by the standardizing population. No value judgements are made as to the 'right' kind of profile.

I think it can be very productive to look upon the ratings of the pedagogical schedules as ipsative scales. The kind of information that a student could derive from the use of these schedules, for example, might be that he or she is more adept at the use of reinforcement than at teaching for concept formation; or that his or her skill at sequencing exemplars in teaching for concept formation is shaky, whereas heightening the salience of the criterial attributes is very satisfactory. I do not suggest that it is realistic to expect all students to achieve perfection on all the items of the schedule, but there is no reason in theory why this should not happen. On the other hand, conventional approaches take it as axiomatic that only a small percentage of all students can or should be allowed to reach the top of the scales. The point of overriding importance, however, is that the score on the ipsative scale indicates to students how they stand on specific aspects of pedagogical theory and practice. Having this information they can decide in consultation with their supervisor whether it is necessary to take action to try to change the shape of the profile and if so, how the job should be tackled.

Many factors will need to be considered by the supervisor before coming to a conclusion as to the best course of action. Many, perhaps most, will be logistical and institutional. But there is a pedagogical consideration that raises some very, very difficult questions for supervisors in today's training institutions. It has to do with cutting scores on the schedules.

Training institutions have come a long way since the early 1970s with regard to this question. Most of them have come to accept that the fine grading that they indulged in in those days when assessing teaching practice was quite illegitimate and naive, and they have moved to a pass/fail method of grading. In my view this is not really logical. If it is difficult or impossible to be certain about cutting scores to sort out the distinction or the credit candidates, how can it be possible to sort out the pass from the fails? In view of some of the incredibly solemn and pompous discussions that go on at final examiners' meetings to decide whether the occasional student is 'just a pass' or 'just a fail', it is clear that many supervisors and examiners still feel the pass/fail distinction to be something special and something about which they have a very special revelatory insight.

In the case of an ipsative scale based on pedagogical schedules, trying to derive a cutting score for pass/fail (i.e. making fine distinctions at an inevitably arbitrary 'pass mark') is even less appropriate. Instead of attempting this, the approach to supervision that I have been arguing for throughout is taken absolutely seriously and all efforts are bent towards helping the students become good teachers rather than on adjudicating between them; and no attempt is made to set cutting scores at the borderline between pass and fail. Two factors referred to in chapter two, in addition to the enormous difficulty of distinguishing genuinely between pass and fail, justify this approach. One is the common observation that by the time students have finished their course as trainee teachers, most unsatisfactory and unsatisfied ones will have dropped out anyway. The second factor, almost certainly a consequence of the first, alluded to previously and less widely realized, is that emerging from the Stones and Webster (1983) survey. This revealed that in Britain very few student teachers fail teaching practice, and of those that do and choose to stay in teaching, almost all pass on a 'resit' within a year, although many will have had little further exposure to formal training. Given this state of affairs, institutions and supervisors should at least examine the proposition that the time, effort and resources expended on the process of attempting to exclude the ugly ducklings is wasted; especially when practically all turn out to be swans anyway.

Experience of dropping this particular pebble in the pool in discussions with teacher educators suggests that the perturbation is likely to be considerable and prolonged. The main overt reaction to the proposal to abandon the process (ritual?) of deciding who shall fail is to raise the banner of defending standards. I have already discussed some of the possible covert reasons. The 'standards' battle-cry is, in fact, a snare and a delusion and, as is the case in discussions about education generally, the loudest cries come from the least well informed. A serious study of research in the field of educational assessment, and particularly in the field of teacher education, I suggest, will lead to the conclusion that the obsessive concern with trying to maintain standards through the juggernaut of most current assessment procedures is more likely to depress standards then elevate them.

This perverse conclusion is based on the arguments re-hearsed earlier about the virtual impossibility of accomplishing the task anyway. But there is more to it than that. There is also an insidious assumption that assessment *by itself* elevates standards, as though measuring their height made children grow. Attention is thus diverted from those aspects of supervision that could really make a difference to student teachers' competence and truly improve standards. The 'standards by assessment' argument actually takes a very negative view of supervision. The emphasis is placed on the spontaneous development of student teachers as they are immersed in the classroom processes. The main function of supervisors in this case is to act as gatekeepers to the profession, and their function as teachers and advisors is devalued. This, of course, is the main burden of the discussion in chapter two of the conflict between student and tutor in practical teaching.

The method of supervision I have described using ipsative

pedagogical schedules takes the view that, by the end of a course of teacher training, students will have had considerable experience of practical teaching based on extensive study of related theoretical principles under the guidance of a supervisor. Unless the training institution is failing in its task badly, all students will have a basic practical competence appropriate to the various stages of the course. Some will decide that teaching is not for them and will leave. However, the basic competence of those graduating should approach (or exceed) that of an experienced teacher. During the course of training, the level of basic competence will be continuously raised in ways that are apparent to, and indeed planned by, supervisor and student. Thus the profile derived from the use of ipsative scales, rather like the scale of values, reveals the personal pattern of emphasis on different aspects of teaching skills, but does not attempt to use the profile to pass judgement on the individual.

Teachers, students, supervisors

There has been little mention of co-operating teachers in this discussion. But clearly everything that has been said about the nature of the relationship between student and supervisor can be said about the teacher in school working with the student. There is a difficult problem at the moment, however. Teachers in schools at present are the prisoners of their past training, which almost certainly provided no introduction to pedagogical theory. They will thus be disadvantaged and less able to assist than if conventional apprenticeship methods are in use. Nevertheless, the experience of a triumvirate working together to solve specific teaching problems can be educative for all its members, and can perform an inservice education function for the teacher. The important thing is to foster the colleaguial relationship referred to, and to attempt to provide systematic inservice training for teachers. However, the provision of pedagogical schedules and access to the arguments sustaining them should be of considerable help in developing the relationship.

For students, pedagogical schedules provide an anchorage for their practical activity and a vital point of contact with teachers and supervisors. Supervisors gain much the same from the common use of schedules. However, they also gain an insight into the effectiveness of their supervision of observing the effect it has on the students' classroom activities and the pupils' contingent learning. In the next chapter I consider the development of instruments to provide even further diagnostic information about the nature of supervision, and also heuristic guides to supervisor action.

7

. . . .

The new supervisor: 1

It is an unfortunate fact that most courses of inservice education and training for experienced teachers parallel those for beginning teachers in their neglect of the study of teaching or pedagogy. Courses abound at master's level in educational studies in various fields such as philosophy, psychology or history of education. There are also courses in a variety of 'main subject' studies, carefully labelled in the style: 'mathematics education' or 'English education' or 'chemical education'; not, note, 'English teaching' or 'maths teaching'. Often educationists outside the training institutions see these courses as academic and hardly relevant to the real world of the classroom. I found this attitude quite prevalent among chief education officers when, as director of an institute of education in a university, I talked to them about courses of inservice training run by the institute. In times of restricted resources these administrators preferred diploma courses in subjects such as remedial education or teaching reading which they saw as 'practical' and likely to have a useful pay-off in terms of actual teaching expertise.

Many teachers have similar views, the flavour of which is suggested by the following imaginary staffroom conversation written by a teacher at the end of a one-year master's course that aimed to be relevant to the needs of practising teachers:

What have you been doing during your year's holiday?

I've been trying to relate my practice as a teacher to psychological principles.

Oh, I did that at college . . . a load of old rubbish. You don't need psychology in the classroom. . . . Do you want coffee or tea?

The course the teacher was referring to was one on pedagogy that I had run for several years and which included a major component devoted to the training of supervisors of student teachers (Stones 1977). The discussion in the pages which follow owes much to that course, through the demands it made upon me to test psychological principles in practice at several levels, through the imaginative work of many of the participating teachers, and not least through the challenges they presented towards the sharpening-up of ideas and hypotheses both in pedagogy and in supervisor training.

Instrumentation of supervision

I have argued in previous pages for a view of supervision as a specific exemplar of the general concept of teaching. I have also argued that principles of pedagogy should not be merely the subject of academic study but that they should be implemented in practical teaching. That is, they should be taken seriously by staff of training institutions as guides to action. It follows, therefore, that logically I should advocate approaches to supervision that incorporate pedagogical principles *and practise them*. In grappling with the problems of employing such an approach in a systematic way, I developed a heuristic guide that extends the work on the instrumentation of pedagogy described in chapter six into the field of supervisor action.

I wish to make clear the difference between this instrument and those described previously. The latter were guides to *teacher* action to enhance *pupil* learning; the former is a guide to *supervisor* action to enhance *student teacher* learning with, of course, the eventual goal of improving pupil learning. Naturally the basic features of the two forms of activity are the same, but the specific working-out of pedagogical principles is different in some particulars, especially those related to dyadic teaching which is common in supervision but rare in teaching. There is also the very important feature of supervision that distinguishes it from all other teaching; it is the only case where *teaching itself* is the subject of study. (I include under the heading of *supervision* all cognate training activities that may have somewhat different titles.) This unique feature of supervision as a form of teaching leads to the complexities of the Chinese box syndrome that I referred to earlier, which nests pedagogical principles within pedagogical principles so that a supervisor may be using notions from concept learning to teach students about reinforcement and principles from reinforcement theory to teach concept learning. These curious matters will be discussed at greater length in due course.

The instrument that provides structure to the process of supervision discussed here is the *Guide for Enhancing Supervision (GES)*. This guide attempts to bring together notions from theory of learning and teaching tempered by practical experience and related to the schedules discussed in the last chapter and the ideas of clinical supervision discussed by workers such as Goldhammer, Blumberg and others and reviewed in detail in Sullivan's monograph (1980). It conceives of supervision as falling into a number of phases as set out in Table 7.1. But although the guide is intended as a focusing device related to counselling a student on a specific piece of teaching, I should like to stress that the successful operation of the instrument depends upon a systematic course such as the one discussed earlier that makes use of the pedagogical schedules. As I said there, students who have not learned the principles embodied in the various items on the pedagogical schedules will be unable to operate with them. Their learning of the principles is, of course, dependent upon their earlier work in pedagogy under the guidance of their supervisors or tutors.

Table 7.1   Guide for Enhancing Supervision

Please note this instrument makes use of the pedagogical schedules I discussed earlier, taken from the book *Psychology of Education: A Pedagogical Approach* (Stones 1979). However, I stress that it is a guide to action not a recipe. Note also that where I have provided examples of supervisor activity, they have been illustrative not prescriptive, and certainly not comprehensive.

Phase 1   Preactive A

1.1   *Decide objective of counselling*
e.g. Students will be able to apply pedagogical principles in a specific teaching activity to satisfy the criteria set out in the pedagogical schedule(s).

1.2   *Ascertain student teacher's initial competence*
e.g. Can students demonstrate knowledge of principles appropriate to the specific teaching task? (Type C skill.) Can students evaluate a piece of teaching of the same type? (Type B skill.)

1.3   *Task analysis*
Identify the schedules appropriate to the projected teaching. Identify specific possible examples of aspects of practical teaching related to the teaching task to use in preliminary discussion with the student teacher.

Phase 2   Interactive A

2.1   Discuss with the teacher the nature of the teaching.

2.2   Encourage the teacher to explore imaginatively ways of implementing pedagogical principles in practice. (Specific examples prepared in 1.3 may be used here.)

2.3   Cue and prompt only as much as is necessary to help the teacher in preparing the lesson. Aim to get the teacher to assume responsibility for his/her own preparation.

2.4   Encourage the teacher in planning the lesson without giving unrealistic or inappropriate feedback.

Phase 3   Preactive B

3.1   *Decide objective(s)*
e.g. The teacher will be able to appraise his/her teaching in the light of pedagogical principles. The teacher will wish to continue the process of self-appraisal with or without the aid of a supervisor.

3.2 *Task analysis*

3.2.1 On the basis of observation of the teacher's performance decide on the nature of the feedback necessary. A recording of the teaching facilitates this task considerably. Specifically identify the strengths and weaknesses of the teaching using the pedagogical schedules as guides.

3.2.2 Identify specific critical incidents in the teaching to use in interactive phase B. Prepare a provisional plan of the counselling session and decide on how to use critical incidents.

Phase 4 Interactive B

4.1 Attempt to establish a positive affective atmosphere. Some suggestions.
Friendly informal tone of voice
Positive opening statements in relation to teaching.
Encouraging nonverbal activities: e.g. smiling, nodding, eye contact.

4.2 Discuss with the teacher the important features of the type of teaching he/she has done. Schedules may be useful here. Prompt and guide as little as possible. Refer back to phase 2.

4.3 Invite the teacher to appraise his/her own performance. How does it compare with the teacher's intentions?

4.4 By prompting and guiding sharpen up the teacher's perceptions of his/her performance.

4.5 By use of video recording (or other record) of critical incidents give feedback at key points. Juxtaposing positive and negative exemplars of the aimed-for activity sharpens up perceptions and reduces negative affect.

4.6 Encourage the teacher throughout to make his/her own analysis and critique based on earlier work in pedagogy.

4.7 Comment approvingly on positive aspects of the teaching.

4.8 Endeavour to get the teacher to identify his/her own

weaknesses and commend for accurate appraisal so neutralizing the negative effects of the identification of shortcomings.

4.9   Avoid criticism unaccompanied by positive suggestions.

4.10 At the end of the counselling session invite the teacher to suggest changes he/she would make if repeating the lesson.

Phase 5 Evaluation

5.1   Ask the teacher to teach another lesson with a similar objective and assess the extent to which improvement has taken place on the various items of the schedule.

5.2   Attempt to assess achievement of affective goals by ascertaining whether the teacher would *voluntarily* wish to be counselled again by the same supervisor.

Obviously 5.2 is particularly difficult to achieve and depends greatly on the relationship built up earlier for a reliable appraisal. A straight question might work on some occasions but subtler approaches are more likely to be needed. Making the counselling voluntary could be very revealing. Anonymous questionnaires to groups might help. Supervisors need to develop a personal psychological robustness when engaging in this type of activity.

A knowledge of pedagogical principles is important not only to provide students with theoretical guides to action, but also because of the effect it has on student/supervisor relationships. Students working within a system of apprenticeship training are totally dependent upon the master teacher or the supervisor; there is little room for discussion or experimentation. The pattern of supervision is likely to be a one-way process with mentor telling learner how to do this, that or the other, commonly without any justifying argument. Justification for a particular course of action is likely to consist of an appeal to experience. One particularly memorable expression in this genre is the one I mentioned earlier (chapter three): 'My teaching mind tells me'. When practical teaching is fully integrated into a course on pedagogy, students tackle the task within a context of previous experience of pedagogical theory and gradual introduction to practice. They thus have a shared field of discourse with their supervisors. Instead of the one-way process – 'Do it this way, that way of the other' – supervisor, student and, if possible, teacher, make a joint attack on the problem of teaching something to someone in the way I described earlier. Thus supervisor/student relationships are transformed from a cloning operation into a co-operative attack on teaching problems.

Although the *Guide for Enhancing Supervision* is centrally related to the approach that I currently see as being most appropriate for improving the effectiveness of supervision, I do not suggest that it is *the definitive* way of operating. As with the pedagogical schedules, *GES* is a heuristic device, a guide to action not a recipe to be followed slavishly. It is important to remember that the object is to enhance supervisors' ability to help student teachers learn how to help pupils to learn. The main thrust of most of the work will, therefore, inevitably be concerned with aspects of psychology of learning. Questions of values and curriculum matters will be discussed in other places, but it seems to me that the important aspect of values as they apply to supervision lies not in any theoretical discussion, but in the way in which supervisors operate. This view is implicit in Blumberg's 'supervisors' houses'. Questions relating to curriculum for a course of teacher training are embodied in the argument I have been making throughout, that current curricula are grotesquely one-sided in their neglect of what surely ought to be absolutely central, namely the study of teaching. Thus my value position and curricular views on the nature of supervision are partially incorporated in the arguments so far enunciated. Obversely I believe that students are likely to be at least as affected by attempts at practical implementation of value positions as by lectures or seminar discussions on the question, although I am convinced that the detached consideration of these questions is also important.

Implementation

In the discussion of this particular approach to supervision I shall follow the overall drift of the schedule since that is the way I think most profitable to proceed at the moment. However, the main framework of the instrument resembles that commonly adopted in clinical supervision so it should be flexible enough to accommodate idiosyncratic adaptations without drastically altering the general line.

The several divisions of *GES* relate to different phases of supervisor action. To some extent they follow conventional practice for clinical supervision, such as the ones mentioned in chapter two suggested by Cogan (1976), the main differences arising from the conceptualization here of supervision as being integrated with theoretical studies in teacher training and therefore able to call upon a shared understanding of pedagogy in supervisor/student teacher discourse.

This orientation is evidenced in the division of the preactive and interactive phases into two parts. The first part is where the supervisor contemplates and plans the optimum approach to the supervisory task before the student teaches. The second is where the supervisor, after having seen the student teach and analysed the performance, plans his or her procedure for the supervisory interview. The same applies to the two aspects of the interactive phases of the supervision.

Preactive A

Perhaps the aspect most prone to personal adaptation is the specification of the objectives of supervision (1.1). In the example I suggest, I have tried to encapsulate in a brief statement a range of complex teacher activities. As I have said earlier, the full implications of these activities can only be understood in relation to the extended discussion of pedagogy that will have taken place in earlier theoretical and practical work. The reference back to the pedagogical schedules provides the supervisor with a good indication of the subordinate elements in the objectives that I have proposed so that it will not be necessary at this stage of counselling to start working out the subobjectives implied by the overall aim since these are already very familiar to supervisor and student. A person deciding upon different overall aims would need to analyse them to identify their component elements as guides to subsequent action, as well as to clarify the understanding of colleagues and students about the detailed nature of the general aims. I believe it possible, however, that even a person with different aims could find the approach to be discussed amenable and useful.

The second element in phase 1 is vital and almost universally neglected in current approaches to supervision. This state of affairs is an inevitable consequence of an apprenticeship approach to teacher training, and obviously the defenders of such an approach would dissent from a view that regards it as important since they expect students to learn teaching skills on the job not beforehand. The suggestion in this section, however, is not that students should be completely competent before they start teaching (who ever is?), but that they will have learned concepts relating to teaching and learning (type C skills) and will have examined and appraised effectively protocol material relating to the teaching of a variety of subjects and groups of learners (type B skills). Supervisors at this stage will be considering the effectiveness of their previous work with students. But they should not rely on orthodox examinations to establish students' competence: this would be worse than useless here. The level of insight shown by students' appraisal of protocol material will provide the best assessment. Clearly this is a matter for the personal judgement of supervisors and once more bespeaks the need for as long term a relationship between supervisor and student as is possible to facilitate this assessment.

The third element in supervisors' preparation is to suggest that they give some thought to the main aspects of student learning upon which they might wish to focus. From earlier acquaintance they will have some idea about those aspects of a student's strengths and weaknesses and may wish to suggest a focus on a particular aspect of teaching, in the teaching under scrutiny, for remedial purposes. Or it may be that the students in a particular group have reached a point in their learning where a specific skill is being accorded special attention. Considerations of this type will orient the supervisor's thinking in attempting to identify the schedule or schedules, or, possibly, just one or two items from a schedule. For example, it is quite feasible that particular consideration may be being given to the evaluation of children's learning and the supervisor would therefore direct the student's attention to those items with particular relevance to that question. In addition it would be necessary to attempt to identify specific exemplars of aspects of the skill or subskill in question, either in recorded protocol form, or print, or raised orally by the supervisor.

This phase is the supervisor's own preparation. The onerousness of the task depends largely on the nature of the course before student teaching takes place. In the case of an integrated course, such as I have suggested, it need not be very onerous since much of the work will already have been done and will merely demand thought about the nature of the specific application.

Interactive A

This phase relates to the preparation for student teaching. It is commonly found in various forms in current courses. The main difference in the operation in the approach under discussion is the appeal to theoretical principles at all stages and the conceptualization of the teaching being prepared for as a joint exploratory operation in pedagogy. Readers familiar with the pedagogical schedules referred to earlier will recognize the elements in this phase. They all relate to theoretical notions from learning psychology. The first element (2.1) does two things. It encourages the student to clarify the nature of the task in hand but, at least as important, it signals the nature of the supervisor/student relationship. The interaction is to be a joint investigation of a pedagogical problem, not a supervisor telling a student how to do it.

The great virtue of embedding this approach in a course such as I have described is that the supervisor can refer to general principles to illuminate particular aspects of the projected teaching because students and supervisor will already have examined these things thoroughly earlier. Further, since all the students working with the supervisor will have a common grounding in pedagogy, the whole of this phase can be handled on a group basis. This is not an exercise in expediency, but a very valuable operation. It chimes completely with the whole argument of this book and the pedagogical schedules. It celebrates the virtues of variety in all spheres of learning.

This procedure differs radically from most current practice. Instead of sorting student teachers into tutorial groups on the basis of their subject of study, a deliberate attempt is made to create supervisory groups that are heterogeneous as to subject and age level of teaching. The rationale for this approach is that the focus of study is *teaching* and not English or maths or eleven years old or fourteen years old. Thus the hetereogeneity of the group forces attention on the essential topic of pedagogy. There is no problem about lack of subject understanding among the different specialists since the level of teaching to which individuals will be aiming is unlikely to be beyond the grasp of their peers; and if it is, the student proposing the teaching should ask him or herself what the implications of this are for the teaching of much less sophisticated learners.

Many years of working in this way have convinced me that it is not only possible but challenging and enjoyable. It can also be very revealing from the epistemological point of view. Frequently in group discussions examining the teaching of particular subjects, students' conceptualization of the structure of their own subject is brought into question. Cherished assumptions about the nature of bodies of theory are shaken and the poverty of some standard textual expositions for school pupils is revealed. It is true that one person's challenge is another person's trauma, but if there are questions to be asked about conventional wisdom on the nature of knowledge in areas of the curriculum I suggest they should be asked, and a group of supportive peers is probably one of the best places for the discussion to take place. I do not suggest, however, that there is no place for individual student/supervisor meetings.

I believe the reasons for the insecure foundations of many student teachers' grasp of the conceptual structure of their subject lie in the way it is taught in schools and higher education. The overwhelming emphasis on expository and transmission teaching, and examinations that hardly ever go beyond the most elementary levels of learning, ensure that little else could be expected. This is not the place to develop this theme, however, though I have done it elsewhere for those interested (Stones 1979).

An interesting specific example of the value of the group work I am suggesting is to be found in an account by Evans (1983) of the development of an honours B.Ed. course which brought together students from the full range of teaching subjects and age levels in a co-operative working group. Their varied interests and backgrounds, being so different, virtually compelled them to focus their attention on common pedagogical concerns when they considered specific teaching problems and developed a new appreciation and understanding of the relationship between pedagogical theory and practice. Another very important benefit accruing from structuring the course in this way, that often exercises the minds of tutors and supervisors, was that it solved some difficult logistical problems inherent in arranging courses in relation to students' specialism. Evans discusses more extensive co-operation among students, a subject that I shall also return to repeatedly.

Within the context of group consideration of the preactive stage of the students' teaching and the supervisor's interactive phase A, as the items in the schedule indicate, the emphasis is on a problem-solving approach and the supervisor's actions are designed to help students tackle pedagogical problems imaginatively and efficiently. Note that the schedule places a great emphasis on enabling the teacher to take an independent line, and although part of the work may go on in the group, the aim is not for students or supervisor to do the work for anyone. There is no contradiction between co-operation and independence.

Foundations of supervision

At this stage of the discussion I am conscious of a problem that arises from current approaches to courses in teacher education. Existing attitudes separate the counselling of student teachers on their teaching from other aspects of their training, whereas in the consideration I have given it so far I have been drawing heavily on understandings and procedures that would have been developed in earlier parts of a course on pedagogy. It seems advisable here, therefore, to devote a little time to considering some of the supervisor activities that lay the foundations for student teaching before we consider the supervisory interview following student teaching itself. I therefore leave the discussion of the remaining aspects of *GES* to the next chapter. Here I should like to consider briefly some things a supervisor might do long before the event to ensure that the supervisor/counselling interview will be a profitable and satisfying experience for both participants.

I refer here to the tutoring of the students prior to their engaging on a piece of practice teaching extending over a number of weeks. Following the general line of the argument so far, the main burden of the meetings at first will be the developing of an understanding of important aspects of pedagogy. This does present difficulties of approach for several reasons, apart from the question of coming to a consensus with colleagues about what the important aspects are. One factor that should not be underestimated is that student teachers, because of their lengthy history of exposure to transmission teaching, where all that there was to it was telling, themselves see little point in discussing pedagogy. They share the simplistic views of a large population in different fields of education and the public. A ploy that I have used that gives insight into students' conceptualizations is to ask them quite simply to explain to their peers how they would set about teaching a particular and quite limited concept to a specific child or group of children. The almost universal reaction is to talk in terms of what they would *tell* the pupils. There is rarely any evidence of student consideration of pedagogical factors. Nor is there ever much understanding of conceptual learning. The students' own concepts about the nature of teaching, acquired over many years of being at the receiving end of a transmission process conducted almost entirely in verbal terms, equate teaching with telling, and competence in learning is measured by the extent to which the learner is able to memorize the words transmitted. I suggest that the process of supervision affords one of the key opportunities for concerned educators to break into this desperately vicious circle.

To illustrate my point, here is an account of a seminar contribution from a student taking a postgraduate course in teacher training. It is taken from a record of the first meeting of the group. I had asked them all to come prepared to explain briefly how they would set about teaching something to someone. They had a completely free choice. The first exposition typified the general character of the contributions. This student teacher was aiming to teach the pupils how to locate a place in an atlas, using the index. His prescription was that he would first tell them this, then that, then the other. End of lesson. For this student there was no problem other than deciding what to tell the pupils. It was, perhaps, an extreme example of transmission teaching but an all too common one, as the students knew from their experiences as pupils in school and undergraduates.

This student had an impatient and sceptical view of pedagogy, which is hardly surprising given the years of experience of transmission teaching to which he had been exposed. It might be of interest and value to readers to have his own account of how he felt at the time.

> Initially I was a non-believer. I couldn't see the relevance of psychopedagogy to myself as a teacher. I now realize that this was due to my lack of understanding of the subject; rather than admit this my natural defence mechanism foolishly dismissed the subject as being unimportant and feeble.

Some other students taking the course in different years had similar views, but in all classes we found that initial hostility gave way to different degrees of enthusiasm almost entirely as a result of finding that the approach actually helped them in their teaching. One other student comment may be adduced to illustrate this point and the way it connects with the apprentice approach:

> The school of my teaching practice was far from easy and at first I did everything as I was told by the established teachers. I did this because at first I did not have the self-confidence to do otherwise. But when I saw I was getting nowhere during the first week or so, I decided to adapt psychopedagogy to the situation I was in and was amazed when I found how much easier it made my task; I also made friends with the children, which was very gratifying.

Clearly one cannot place too much reliance on student self-report even when anonymity is permitted, but there is a fair number of straws in this particular wind and I shall return to different aspects of student teachers' reactions later.

I believe this digression is relevant to our consideration of the task of supervision in the preparatory stages leading to school practice. The initial problems may appear to be at times, and no doubt are, very great, so the knowledge that they are probably transitory is important information to supervisors. To give some indication of a way of proceeding that encourages a different way of looking at pedagogy I consider points made by various student teachers and examine the example given above to illustrate one approach to opening students' eyes to the need to consider pedagogical factors in planning and teaching lessons.

In the example discussed above I raised with the students questions about the nature of the entry competence of the pupils. Are they able to use an index? Are they familiar with the use of co-ordinates? Is the student teacher clear about the way in which learning is to be evaluated? Is it to be by asking the pupils questions? Should these be written or oral? Or are they to be asked to locate places in the atlas in question and other atlases? Concerning the task itself, if the pupils have the entry competences referred to, then the task is relatively simple, it is just a question of asking them to apply two already existing skills to a new situation. Perhaps all that would be necessary would be to remind them of the use of an index and co-ordinates. If the pupils have neither of the two skills then a very important question arises: is it more appropriate to attempt to teach them the two skills in this very specific context to solve the very specific problem, or would it be better to teach them the skills for general application? If the latter, then the proposed lesson is called into question. In this case the use of an index in the atlas would be just one exemplar in the teaching of the general principles of index usage, and the use of co-ordinates to locate places in an atlas would be just one exemplar in teaching the principles of the use of co-ordinates. In the teaching of the skills of using an index and using co-ordinates, notions from the psychology of concept learning would be relevant and would enable the teacher to make sure that the pupils would acquire skills of general application so that a lesson solely on the use of an index in an atlas could well be necessary, since all the pupils would have to do to find a place would be to deploy existing general skills.

It will come as no surprise to readers that in the case in question the student had considered none of these things. And indeed, why should he? He was entering a new field about which he was ignorant. Indeed, he was ignorant that the field existed. But the examination of these problems in discussion, while it aroused interest and the beginnings of conviction in other students, was rejected by the student in question with a fine display of cognitive dissonance evidenced by his comments.

The thing that really convinced this student and all the others in different groups was the experience of tackling real teaching problems, and the message that comes across very clearly from course evaluation is that it is very important to dovetail the theory and the practice of pedagogy right from the beginning. But the practice needs to be related to the aspects of theory under consideration at the time, and not at some time in the future. It does not need to be an extended period but merely an opportunity to test the relevance and effectiveness of specific pedagogical procedures as they arise in theoretical discussions. An alternative approach, of course, could reverse the sequence and take up theoretical aspects of pedagogy as a consequence of tackling practical teaching problems. My own preference when beginning a course is to take a structured approach to theory that goes out to the classroom within the first few weeks following preparatory work on theoretical principles, but I do not suggest there is any one correct prescription in these matters.

However, it is probably productive to give students some overview of the nature of the pedagogy the supervisor is to espouse during the course, and to get the students to do some reading about the subject and introduce it to seminar discussions. But from the outset it is absolutely vital to avoid transmission teaching. Students are not learning *about* pedagogical principles, but *how to use them* in teaching. Supervisors using the same pedagogical principles will avoid mere verbalizing and will therefore introduce into discussions, at a very early date, examples of aspects of real teaching to exemplify the concepts and principles they are considering. The examples, although of *real teaching*, need not necessarily be in the classroom. Recordings of various types, video, audio, film or printed transcripts are all possible devices to help build up students' concepts about teaching. But there should be no question of this material being just *stuck on* to a supervisor's lecture. It must be integral to it. I can illustrate this by referring back to a point made earlier. Teaching the concept of reinforcement in the classroom, I have used videotape extracts of a variety of different teachers in different classrooms, selected to provide different exemplifications of the same general principles. The supervisor's role in the use of this material is to help students identify the common defining attributes of the concept (not to tell them what they are) and to realize that lessons differing widely as to style and method may well be very similar in regard to the teachers' use of reinforcement. Obviously material of this kind can be used to enrich students' learning of other pedagogical skills.

As soon as possible the same type of material should be used as protocols. Now, instead of the supervisor using the material structured to enhance the learning of the skills in question, it is used as material for the students to scrutinize and appraise in the light of the principles they have learned earlier. In this way they enhance their grasp of those principles, and also lay the ground for the appraisal of their own teaching which is so vital for their continuing self-development after completing training. If experiences of short pieces of teaching are dovetailed in at this stage, the students can use their own teaching as protocol material quite early in the course, an experience which has a powerful effect on their interest in and commitment to pedagogy.

Other factors which helped students in their preparation for teaching were the schedules which oriented them and enabled them to approach their teaching in a systematic way without constraining them. They also undoubtedly provided a crucial frame of reference for talking about problems of specific teaching projects. Later a project which demanded that they write an extensive report of a lesson, in which they reviewed the literature on the subject and its teaching, prepared a pedagogical analysis, taught and recorded the lesson, reviewed the lesson, analysed it and critically appraised it, provided an exacting but highly productive and illuminating experience. Other aspects of preparation for teaching will be discussed later as they seem particularly relevant. But perhaps the most important general point to make about the preparation is to take up point 2.2 and apply it seriously to the whole process of teaching students about pedagogy. The process of supervision is then seen as a challenging business taken to be a complex form of teaching, the implementing of which is best to be found in imaginative approaches to developing courses in which practical teaching activities and discussion of principles merge into one process.

8

. . . .

The new supervisor: 2

In the cosmology of supervision the approach expounded here approximates more to the continuous creation than the big bang paradigm. But it is almost certain that the adherents to the latter considerably outnumber those of the former. A typical exposition of the dominant paradigm is presented by Diamonti (1977) writing about a 'reappraisal of student teaching'. He sees it as '*the culmination* of a student's training, *it is an opportunity to put theory into practice* and to develop and demonstrate the qualities thought necessary to become a teacher' (my italics). Yet here we are two-thirds of the way through the book and only just getting to the nub of the matter.

And unrepentant. I do not for one moment wish to single out Mr Diamonti for particular reproach for the statement quoted could have been written by numerous authors in this field. However, his statement does encapsulate so many of our problems. For a year or two supervisors wind up the students with theory, then comes the moment when the spring is released and off they go practising. In fact there is as much chance of students in such situations spontaneously incorporating the theory they have come across into their practice as there is of a clockwork toy explaining the laws of physics that endow it with movement. In fact Diamonti himself, apparently unwittingly, identifies the greatest obstacle of all to such an occurrence: that practical experience in teacher training is an apprenticeship system. His proposal for reappraisal is that this fact should be recognized, the supervisor phased out of the system and the students handed over to master teachers.

Supervisors taking this view will be impatient with the

tedious approach to what they see as the culmination of student teacher training taken here. They will wish to get on with the real job and put the students in front of the pupils so that they, or master teachers, can demonstrate or remonstrate about how to teach. I hope that the matters we are now to consider will at least give the reader pause to think about the desirability of procedures of this type. But even now we must leave many supervisors champing at the bit because, although the lesson has been planned and taught, there is still one more stage before the student and supervisor actually sit eyeball to eyeball to talk about it.

Preactive B

The point is that precounselling preparation is no less crucial than the other stages in the process of supervision. Traces of it are likely to be found in most cases where a form of counselling follows student teaching. But in clinical counselling as adapted here it cannot be vestigial. It is an exacting and time-consuming task demanding a high level of pedagogical knowledge and professional expertise. The conceptualizing of the aims of the counselling session mentioned in *GES* demands this, and also a clarification of the affective intentions of the supervisor. This conceptualization, however, embodies the supervisor's values and aspirations and will probably arise naturally from them with little need for preparation. The other matters are different. Although the general ideas about such things as feedback, task analysis and identification of critical incidents will not be novel, the specific application of those ideas in the supervisory interview will be new and unique because they relate to unique examples of teaching by the student.

A supervisor will be helped enormously in preparing for the counselling session by some form of recording of the student's teaching. With the wide availability of video recording equipment, it is now possible to make such recordings without undue difficulty. Failing video, audio recordings, and failing those, a detailed written record of the progress of the lesson should be made. These recordings are the essential raw material for the fashioning of the supervisor's approach to the counselling session with the student. Although there is no suggestion that recordings should take the place of direct observation, they provide opportunities for the observation and analysis of teaching otherwise completely impossible. The supervisor uses the record of the student teacher's teaching as a protocol, in the way described earlier, to make a personal appraisal of the teaching, and notes those points that seem to merit particular comment. The aim of all the recordings will be to avoid preoccupation with the cosmetic aspects of the teaching and to focus on the pedagogical aspects. The supervisor's notes will record carefully the locations, in the recording of the teaching, of incidents that highlight particularly interesting points in the student's attempted exemplification of pedagogical principles. The analysis upon which this record depends will naturally identify those features of the student's teaching the supervisor wishes to comment on, and will facilitate the preparation of a plan for the counselling session.

The plan itself needs to be thought out in some detail in view of the complexity of the operation. As I sought to point out earlier, the counselling encounter is an unusually complex form of teaching, therefore, I suggest, it needs particularly careful preparation. In line with the aims of the operation, one of the tasks of the supervisor will be to help the student towards self-appraisal, using the recording as a sort of personal protocol. This is difficult enough, but in addition careful attention must be paid to the affective side in view of the delicacy of dyadic encounters and the potential for creating unintentional negative affect. Hence the need throughout the course of teacher training for the appraisal of protocol material to be objectified, so that at the counselling stage the student will have some chance of viewing the recording as *the* teaching rather than *my* teaching. Handling discussions aimed to foster this objectivity demands sensitivity and careful preparation. I, therefore, recommend supervisors' notes that cover every step in the counselling process. Not, I hasten to add, a script to be read come what may, but a guide to action so that nothing important will be overlooked and the general line thought out coolly beforehand will be followed and not abandoned in the heat of the moment.

The preparation of the plan of action for the counselling session will be facilitated by a glance ahead at the likely general lines of proceeding established on previous occasions, or through consideration of pedagogical principles. I have set out some items of guidance in phase four of *GES* and readers will find in them some indication of an orientation toward the counselling meeting that might be borne in mind at the planning stage. The marrying of any appropriate items on this part of the schedule with the specific details of preparation will help to clarify the needed supervisory action to achieve particular ends. Clearly one's operating with such an approach is a learning process that will be modified with experience and may lead to modification in the planning for counselling. But if the modification is to be productive it is necessary to keep careful account of the moves that suggest the need for future change, and the items on the different parts of the schedule may provide guidance for effecting productive changes.

At this stage it may be of interest to readers to consider the report of an experienced teacher, taking a course on supervision, on his analysis of a counselling task. He had gone through the counselling steps we have been discussing and he is now preparing for the counselling session. The report is rather lengthy so I quote selections and précis others:

> After a rather intensive study of the video and audio recordings of the student's lesson, from a number of different angles, I had built up a large amount of data, all potentially usable in the counselling session. It was particularly striking how much my original impression of the teaching was modified. First impressions are clearly not a good foundation for counselling. Successive scrutinies of the lesson made the task of counselling increasingly forbidding, since the weaknesses (in the teaching) were many. The whole task began to take on a new significance. If an honest appraisal of the lesson were to be given, the impact on the student was likely to be very damaging to her confidence. The dilemma for a supervisor is obvious. How is he to voice his criticisms and yet be constructive?

In view of the many problems identified in the student's teaching the supervisor thought that it would be a mistake to take a broadly based approach and instead decided to focus on one or two particularly important points. He decided that the student's weaknesses arose mainly from faulty task analysis of the lesson and insufficient clarity in her analysis of the concept she was trying to teach. He located various places in the recording of the lesson to exemplify, in short extracts of about thirty seconds, aspects of the main areas he thought suitable to comment on and use as positive or negative exemplars of the concepts he was trying to teach. *The Schedule for the Teaching of Concepts* discussed in chapter six was to be used in conjunction with the recording to focus the counselling session:

> The final act of preparation for the counselling was to comb the whole lesson, together with such impressions as I had picked up in conversation with the student, to find something about which I could say positive encouraging things. This proved difficult; there was the obvious need to avoid over-enthusing about relatively insignificant things. Perlberg and Theodor (1975) reveal teacher-counsellees' distaste for that kind of supervisory behaviour. In the event certain positive points were made.

In fact the supervisor identified the student's air of confidence, her sense of direction and purpose, and her ability to tune in to the cultural wavelength of the pupils. He then drew up a plan for the counselling session and noted these points as providing a suitable opening gambit for the session. He wrote down the comments he would be likely to make and the general orientation of his remarks. He also noted the danger that supervisors trying to teach their students might fall into an expository mode and finish up *telling* the student thus effectively ensuring that the objective of enabling the student to become an autonomous, self-monitoring, self-critical teacher would *not* be achieved. The notes for the counselling session go as follows:

PLAN FOR COUNSELLING SESSION:
LESSON ON 'SCALE'

(1) Focus on positive points: my first impression of your *style*

  – air of confidence
  – sense of direction and purpose
  – ability to tune in to the cultural wavelength of the pupils.

These things important, particularly empathy with pupils: if you have this ability you start with a definite advantage. Your sense of direction means that you are not likely to become submerged in the ebb and flow of the lesson.

(2) Your problem now is to stand back from the lesson and appraise it *objectively*, on what basis? Whether the structure and methods were appropriate to what you were aiming to do.

(3) How do you think the lesson went? (Expect comments re artificiality and re need to keep going regardless.)

(4) Refer to some of the questions indicated in 'guiding thoughts' (given to student beforehand to orient her thinking about the teaching). What about the participation of the pupils in the lesson? Could you have arranged things so that they took more part and with more chance of success?

(5) Focus on lesson objectives: ask for definition (praise if identified).
Use video clips 1 and 2: what particular difficulties were *anticipated* or *inherent*? (e.g. vocabulary: *scale* any possible confusion with other meanings? *drawing to scale, scaled down, in proportion*?)

(6) Call to mind idea of *task analysis*.
Can you see (from video clips 6, 1 and 2) that you have two objectives? (Idea of *scale* in scale drawing, a concept; and the idea of *drawing to scale*, a skill based on certain principles.) (Show clip 7 which indicates pupils' confusion.)

(7) Ask: what steps are needed (in teaching concept of scale)? Show as example my idea of the breakdown of the concept of scale. (Criterial attributes: all features of *angle* the same; all features of *line* reduced or expanded in proportion.) Detailed analysis of what pupils would need to *know*. (Show clip 5 to illustrate how teacher's assumptions can go wrong and what they would be able to do.) Sequence the learning in naturally graded steps, not too big.

(8) Choice and use of exemplars (to help pupils see criterial attributes) and non-exemplars (to enable better discrimination). Look at the non-exemplars which were chosen and ask their purpose (e.g. things drawn to actual size; use of classroom drawings). Did you learn anything from this? What might have been a good pre-entry test?

(9) Separate out the two objectives (see point six). Why not use knowledge of *scale* as prequisite for lesson on drawing to

scale? Show two other examples of task analyses. Suggest student should make a task analysis of teaching this skill, including in it arrangements for providing feedback for you and the pupils.

(10) Possible conclusion (on positive note again). This kind of task analysis is a preliminary but essential step onto which you can build the positive qualities we have noticed in the lesson, i.e. a good relationship with the pupils and a general awareness and sense of purpose. How would you teach the lesson if you had to do it again?

Since the notes were a working guide for an individual supervisor they are understandably elliptical, but I hope they convey an accurate flavour of the nature of the preparation and its unsuspected complexities. Note particularly the point about the gradual realization of the deficiencies in the lesson. Only the scrutiny of the teaching using the recording and the schedule revealed the problems. I suggest that this illustrates the generally simplistic way in which supervision is regarded. In the absence of analytical tools problems are undetected; teaching is hardly ever properly scrutinized except at the most global level.

Another example of a note of preparation may add a little more to the reader's understanding of this approach to supervision, this time one that I used with an experienced teacher who had taught a lesson in a course on economics for students in further education. I choose this example for several reasons, perhaps the most important one being the point I have made repeatedly, that the provision of a variety of exemplars is essential to concept learning, and the consistent argument that the teaching of different subjects and to different age levels is all teaching and should employ the same basic pedagogical principles even though its different manifestations may differ in non-criterial specifics.

The lesson was a difficult one to advise on for more than one reason. A key factor is the tradition in further education for the teachers to teach mainly by exposition. The job is not made easier by the fact that examining bodies often make what I think is an uninformed attempt to apply control to courses by the imposition of teaching objectives lock-stepped to specific weeks in the course. The effect is for teachers to divide up the syllabus into sections and 'do' the appropriate amount per week, mainly by transmission methods. 'It's the only way of covering the syllabus.' Not, I realize, a situation unique to further education, but more virulent there than elsewhere. The teaching was a very thoroughly prepared example of its kind, and, in view of the arguments advanced throughout this book, the reader will realize the nature of the problem: how to help her to consider other ways of grappling with the task without being so negative as to put her off completely, a particularly difficult task with an experienced teacher.

The notes, again, are somewhat elliptical. The italicized parts are reminders to the supervisor of the actions that may be helpful at the time; the remainder are reminders of the kind of thing he might say. The counselling, in fact, was not only to be recorded, but to take place in front of a group of other experienced teachers studying supervision. S = supervisor; Q = question.

PLAN FOR COUNSELLING SESSION ON TEACHING OF A LESSON ON BUDGET

General supportive chat: first of the group to be counselled: was she very nervous? Were the students (when they were recorded)? What about the cosmetic effect? Nice episode at beginning with group joking, etc. *Eye contact: S attends: leans towards: shows opening of lesson on video.*

Q What do you think about it? How do you think it went in general?

Encourage by nonverbals. Be prepared to probe when necessary.

Can we be more specific and relate it to *STOC* or pedagogy in general?

Encourage and probe.

I think you certainly did some of the things very clearly. (Orienting and preliminary idea – simplified examples – using their own budgets.)

Show second clip.

Now like to look at the general approach. Look at a typical example.

Third clip. Basic budget balancing.

Can you explain how this approach relates to idea of concept learning?

I wonder about exemplars and non-exemplars? About criterial and non-criterial attributes? How did these relate to your
question papers (used in the teaching)?
Encourage and probe.
I wonder if the concept is more than budget? Is it a higher
order concept? (She seemed to be talking about the use of
fiscal measures to manipulate the economy.) What do you
think?
Invite, be receptive.
Can we turn to key element in learning discussed last week?
Feedback. How do you think you fared with this? (The point
was that she gave completely non-specific feedback
throughout: the group answered together, she replied 'yes'.)
Show fourth clip, showing group answers. Invite comments.
Look at a later section in the same clip where this problem
was particularly striking.

Planning continued in this vein and S noted key points to
use in a summing-up. The plan concluded with the viewing of
the end of the lesson, with the group breaking up and relaxing.
S to comment on this in an attempt to close on a positive note.
Then S to ask how she would tackle it if she were to teach the
same lesson again. S concludes by commending her perception
and suggestions for improvement.

Hoagy Carmichael used to sing a song: 'Accentuate the
positive, eliminate the negative'. This is what both the
supervisors in the extracts quoted tried to do in their planning.
But they also tried to help the teachers towards a rigorous
analysis and appraisal of their own teaching. Hence the
repeated references to inviting the teacher to make her own
comments, and the probing aimed at getting her to bring to
mind pedagogical principles that might have helped her to
solve the teaching problem she was faced with. Let us now
consider how a supervisor might put the counselling plan into
action.

Interactive B

In many training institutions this phase of supervision will
only occur when the student teacher has embarked upon a
period of practice extending over several weeks. In Britain it
may be a 'short practice' of three or four weeks, and this could

well be fairly near the beginning of the course. But there is no reason at all why this should be so. It could be introduced, as I have suggested earlier, more gradually and, in fact, it would be if the integrated approach to pedagogy and teacher training I have been advocating were to be adopted. There is an important reason for making this comment here. A supervisor's job in counselling a student who has not had the gradual introduction to teaching is likely to be more difficult and more stressful for both participants than if the experience had been prepared for and phased in gradually. The general approach of the counselling sessions, however, will be the same, but both will differ from conventional approaches in their basis in theoretical principles.

Present staffing arrangements in training institutions in Britain may contribute to problems in the phasing in of students to practical teaching. Frequently several different members of the teaching staff will be tutoring a student on different aspects of theory and practice. The development of a wider interest in pedagogy might make it possible for individual tutors to combine some of the functions currently shared among two or more. If this is not practicable, it is very important that staff co-operate and communicate so as to facilitate the gradual phasing in I referred to above.

In the counselling session, general principles of pedagogy are supplemented by specific ideas from counselling practice and clinical supervision, as discussed in chapter two. There is, however, no suggestion of therapy merely because counselling notions are used. The spirit that informs the meeting is of the joint examination of an attempt to tackle a teaching problem which both participants have considered earlier. It is an exploration of the effectiveness of the student's teaching in which the supervisor takes the main part, by virtue of greater acquaintanceship with theoretical principles and practical teaching, including the work of previous generations of student teachers. But even though both may well have been parties to the planning of the teaching, it is likely that the student will feel vulnerable, particularly if this is an examination of the first extended piece of teaching to be attempted. Thus anything the supervisor can do to create a positive affective climate should be done, and this is where the ideas from counselling come in.

A useful and convenient source for some key ideas on counselling as they may apply to teaching is to be found in Ivey (1974b). It is not always clear just how he sees the application of these ideas. At times he seems to be referring to student teacher counselling and at times he seems to be discussing the training of teachers as counsellors. However, the drift of his paper can readily be interpreted as applicable to our present concerns. He identifies what is a crucial skill for the counsellor/supervisor, the ability to listen. The central behavioural components of listening are: 'eye contact (if you talk with someone, look at them), physical posture (assume an attentive posture, be relaxed), and verbal following behaviour (don't change the topic but stay with the other person).'

Ivey suggests a number of skills that are relevant to student teacher counselling. A first cluster is a group of skills intended to help a supervisor start an interview and focus on how to get another person to talk freely and fully. The skills comprise attending behaviour and open-ended questions allied to minimal cues such as nodding or short statements intended to keep the other person talking. A second cluster relates to listening skills and the development of sensitivity to the interviewee's emotional state. The latter is clearly of prime importance in the highly charged supervisory interview. Unfortunately, as Ivey remarks, some counsellors never learn the skill. In some cases of student teacher supervision it is highly likely that the question is never considered, and even if it were, it might well, in the extreme case, be thought irrelevant. However, for those readers who take a different view it is possible, once one is aware of it, to practise the skill and improve one's sensitivity to the student's emotional state and so improve one's counselling. The cognitive analogue to the last skill is being sensitive to the essential content of what the other person is saying. Picking up these points and paraphrasing them helps students to clarify their ideas.

The schedule *Guide for Enhancing Supervision* assimilates ideas such as these, together with aspects of clinical supervision, to those from the field of pedagogy so as to provide a composite instrument that makes a number of specific suggestions for the guidance of supervisors. The *Guide* has been used and refined in supervision and the training of supervisors so that one hopes readers will find it of value and at least an indication of the way they may proceed themselves. The suggestions aimed at creating a positive emotional climate involve the supervisor in trying to put the student at ease. A relaxed open manner can be expressed in the supervisor's bodily movements or posture. Two easy chairs at about ninety degrees to each other are almost certainly better than two upright chairs on opposite sides of a table. Leaning towards the student rather than away signals an interest in the student's account of the way the teaching went and why. Nonverbal signals such as smiling and nodding, paraverbals such as noises of approval, and verbal reinforcers such as approbatory comments and picking up remarks made by the student and *reflecting* or paraphrasing them approvingly, all help in establishing an atmosphere that will permit genuine learning to take place.

But the object of the exercise is not just to make students feel good, the hope is that the discussion will make better teachers. So supervisors need to be sharp and probing as well as warm and supportive, and this is where the preparation of the preceding months and the preactive thought given before the counselling come in. The counsellor's teaching plan is now to be implemented.

In the best case interview, the teaching plan would be virtually redundant. The student teacher would make a critique of the teaching that the supervisor would recognize as at least as valid and as competent as the one the supervisor had made in preparation for the session, and all that would remain to be done would be to express agreement and delight. In the average case this is not likely to happen but it's as well to bear in mind that it could, if only to help one keep in the front of one's mind that the aim is to get the student to carry out the analysis and critique and only to intervene when essential. In the worst case it is no less essential to resist the temptation to *tell* when what is needed is help to build up the student's autonomy.

I suggest that the best case is one that we should aim for for all students. Thus throughout the interview we should be open and inviting, encouraging the student to comment and appraise. What one is doing here is trying to help the student view the teaching as protocol material for the kind of appraisal that students and supervisor have been making throughout the course. Only when difficulties arise and important points are missed should the supervisor intervene, and then with questions which probe and demand thought about the pedagogical validity and effect of specific aspects of the teaching. It is at moments like this that the recordings of the teaching will be particularly useful. This is where the supervisor makes use of the critical incidents identified in the preactive stage. All that is needed is to view a short sequence of the teaching, repeatedly if necessary, for the student to appraise and comment on. Let us bear in mind here the comment made by the first supervisor mentioned above, that repeated viewing brings out aspects of teaching overlooked at first and modifies one's appraisal of it. Where there is difficulty the supervisor will prompt, guide and encourage the student to call to mind the relevant pedagogical principles that will help to shed light on the issue in question.

It may be that some of these critical incidents will refer to negative aspects of the student's performance and such episodes will need particularly sensitive handling by the supervisor. The problem is to give realistic feedback without making the student feel shattered. Of course, if there is a generally positive affective atmosphere in the meeting and if the student/supervisor relationship is of fairly long standing, and especially if it has involved the kind of preparation for practical teaching discussed in earlier chapters, the problem may well be minimal. However, experience of grappling with the problem in supervisor training suggested the need for item 4.9 in the *GES* schedule as a guide to supervisor action that has been found successful. It demands skill of the supervisor in guiding the discussion and probing so that the student sees the point and makes a self-critical appraisal. It is a key supervisory skill that merits practice. This is another point at which a common understanding of pedagogical principles and the use of schedules such as those mentioned in earlier chapters is quite crucial. Without them it will be difficult, if not impossible, to objectify the critical comments and discuss them coolly as *the* teaching rather than *my* or *your* teaching in the way students have discussed protocols previously.

Supervisors operating in the way I have suggested may, at times, encounter two somewhat problematic types of student reaction. The first is when the student thinks that the lesson went very well, when, in fact, that was by no means the case. The other reaction is when the student thinks the whole exercise was so awful that there is no hope of improving. I believe that these two extremes are unlikely to occur if the practical teaching is embedded in a course on pedagogy such as I have been discussing. If they do, or some similar if less extreme reaction occurs, I find that gentle probing along the lines of the schedule can redress the balance towards realism. If the counselling also takes place in the context of a supportive group these problems can be reduced or eliminated whilst not being ignored or glossed over.

Readers will recognize aspects of counselling skill embodied in the schedule, *GES*. Other aspects owe much of their rationale to the pedagogical schedules referred to earlier. All the time the emphasis is on encouraging student teachers to analyse their own teaching in the light of principles related to effective human learning, and to use that knowledge to identify its strengths and weaknesses and propose ways of improving it. *Telling* students what their deficiencies are is of doubtful value and its probable main effect will be to produce negative affect and unaccepting attitudes in the students. More complete information about the pedagogical aspects will be found by referring to the various schedules and the book from which they are derived (Stones 1979).

The final phase of supervision, *evaluation*, chimes with the formative approach to supervision rather than the summative one. The final climactic assessment, often with an 'external' present, is no place for the kind of activity I have been discussing. To my mind, that type of assessment is virtually an exercise in sterility for reasons I have rehearsed in some detail earlier. Apart from such eccentric exercises, supervisors are likely to be interested in whether or not their efforts have borne any fruit. What better way to find out than to see the teacher teach another similar lesson. In formative evaluation this is possible and, taking a pedagogical approach, it will have benefits beyond the improvement of one particular lesson. I am not unaware of the logistical contraints that beset such operations, but suggest that it is worth an effort to mount in view of the potentially rich feedback in this activity.

On the affective side, the last item of all in the schedule, would the student *voluntarily* wish to be counselled again, is most telling and can be salutary for the supervisor. But since the student teachers are putting themselves on the line all the time in the supervisor's appraisal of their teaching, perhaps there is a certain equity in this item. I have experienced negative replies myself and found that I learned things about my supervision from discussing this kind of reaction that helped on later occasions, despite the negative supervisory affect aroused. One important lesson may be exemplified by an encounter at the end of which the student teacher reported feeling depressed about the whole business, and on reviewing my counselling I realized that I had concentrated on points for improvement and neglected to remark on the positive features of the lesson. All my experience of analytical scrutiny of teaching as it is demonstrates that this is an almost universal problem and is certainly one that supervisors need to be aware of. Of course, the degree of trauma one experiences when discovering such things about one's supervision depend almost entirely on the supervisor/student relationship and the relationships within the group of students one is involved with. With friendly relationships it could be very little and, if the group is accustomed to working together, the members can help each other and their supervisors to improve their work.

Group supervision

A little earlier I referred to a supervisory session that was taking place in a group situation. This is an approach that I have found particularly helpful, if somewhat traumatic at first, in developing in the students the ability to look at examples of teaching relatively objectively and without too intense a feeling of personal threat. But of course, as I have repeatedly stressed, the degree of anxiety in situations like these is less, and the benefit students derive from them is far greater, if such procedures are part of the normal tutorial routine. In the type of teacher training I have envisaged so far, there would have been a gradual build-up to this kind of activity that would, to a great extent, defuse it and render it less traumatic. The session involves the supervisor counselling students in supervisory group meetings. It is a genuine counselling interview but with the student's colleagues unobtrusively present. The planning of the counselling is done by the supervisor so that he or she is much better prepared for the session than the observers and so, strictly speaking, it is group observation of counselling rather than group counselling. However, although the counselling planned by the counsellor at the preactive stage is implemented in a dyadic interview, the observers, the student and the supervisor all join in a group discussion afterwards.

The benefits of sessions of this type are many and varied. Teaching at different levels is being brought under scrutiny. Since the supervisor will have used recorded material of the student teaching the pupils in the counselling, the students will be able to appraise their colleague's teaching and compare their appraisals with those of the supervisor, of the other students in the group and, of great importance, with the student who did the teaching. At another level the group, supervisor as well as students, will be able to discuss the supervision and examine the extent to which it exemplifies the pedagogical practices that it preaches. Note that, in doing this, the students are making particularly complex appraisals of their peer's teaching. They are appraising the teaching and the supervisor's appraisal of the teaching and drawing conclusions about it. To do this effectively demands very high-level activity and understanding of theoretical principles. Group discussion under the general guidance of the supervisor can foster the ability to make such appraisals.

Meetings such as this demonstrate particularly obviously the poverty of atheoretical approaches to teaching. With no grounding in pedagogy there would be practically nothing to talk about and the group exchanges would be more akin to coffee table chat than rigorous explorations of the highly complex phenomena that constitute teaching. The cynic might say that this is the reason why such sessions are rarely found. And, of course, it cannot be denied that the supervisor who indulges in the kind of activity advocated here is well on the way to relinquishing the normal supervisory role of oracular expositor. I imagine that this is an abrogation unlikely to assume epidemic proportions in the foreseeable future; but one hopes.

A supervisor aspiring to operate in this way would naturally work towards such supervisory sessions through the type of activity I have discussed earlier so that in many ways the sessions would be an integral part of the course. This integration is important not only for conceptual and pedagogical reasons but also for logistical ones. The careful preparation for and execution of supervision described here are, obviously, much more time-consuming than the fleeting visit so often encountered. The integration of the theoretical aspects of the course with the practical helps overcome this problem. Group work also helps considerably by providing a richness of focused appraisal of teaching that reduces the number of times a supervisor needs to engage in the kind of detailed operation outlined here. I should point out, however, that the counselling session itself need not be, perhaps should not be, too lengthy.

Outcomes

To illustrate the effect of this approach to supervision I return to the earlier discussion of the supervisor's counselling the student teacher on teaching a lesson on scale, since I think readers might find interest and enlightenment in its outcome.

Recall the supervisor's first reaction was reasonably favourable and then, after viewing the recording of the lesson once or twice, he found his opinion changing and wondered how he could best tackle the counselling so as to have a positive effect and help the student. Now let us consider the student teacher's evaluation of the teaching:

The lesson as a whole had one major fault and that was in the analysis of the teaching task. When originally devising the lesson the main objective was seen to be the teaching of the concept of scale, but the many parts of this concept were not considered in enough detail. The concept of scale was taken to include recognizing objects drawn to scale from non-exemplars and drawing an object to scale. This, however, involved two quite separate concepts. The first involved the pupils understanding the concept of scale, the second was the task of drawing an object to scale. The lesson was originally planned to develop the pupils' understanding of scale and the drawing of an object was seen as a useful way of evaluating pupils' understanding. The problems arose, however, because each concept requires a different set of skills and techniques . . .

The task of teaching the pupils to draw an object to scale was not considered at all within the teaching task analysis. The ability to draw an object to scale was seen as a spin-off from the teaching of the concept. This is mainly where the lesson was unsuccessful. The drawing of an object to scale was seen as a good evaluation of how well the pupils had understood the concept. Their failure to do this successfully did not, however, prove conclusive. Their lack of ability to complete this task effectively may have resulted just as much from their lack of ability to draw to scale as it did from their lack of understanding of the concept of scale. Thus if the lesson was to be repeated it would be necessary to break down the task further . . .

Although a pretest was given, this was merely to try to ascertain the degree of difficulty the pupils could cope with and it did not contain any of the subordinate concepts that would be necessary to the lesson. A better test could have been devised to include some of the necessary words and terms, for example *rectangle* and *proportion* . . .

The failure to analyse the teaching task fully shows itself clearly in the use of exemplars and non-exemplars throughout the lesson. (Student quotes various instances.) The exemplar of a football pitch demonstrated its lack of suitability in two ways. First it was expected that the pupils would know immediately its actual size. They did not. This exemplar, which was aimed at relating the lesson content to things the pupils were familiar with, therefore did not succeed. (Quotes exchange with pupils: estimate pitch seven yards long.)

The student goes on to discuss the effects of inadequate task analysis on the whole approach to teaching the concept and its effect on other aspects of the teaching, including reinforcement:

In evaluating the lesson it became apparent that there was very little actual reinforcement, particularly in the case of teacher approval or praise for an action. In only one instance was direct praise given for a pupil's correct answer. The lack of this type of reinforcement arose because it depended upon another type of reinforcement, that of success for the pupils. A large part of the lesson built up in stages. It depended upon success at one stage before the next stage could be approached. Thus if the pupils did not succeed at the initial stage they would not obtain reinforcement because of their lack of success.

This student's realization of the essentiality of adequate task analysis and ascertainment of pupils' baseline competence is a common outcome of the appraisal by student teachers of their teaching using the guidelines of the pedagogical schedules. The schedules do not create the problems, they give the students tools to help them perceive and tackle them. The realization at this stage in her career that she barely reinforced the pupils is something that many teachers never grasp throughout their whole careers and much the same can be said about the ignoring of baseline competence, for which assertion I draw on repeated observation of established teachers going through similar experiences as this student. The further understanding that the pedagogical structure of the lesson was a causative factor for the lack of reinforcement is a particularly important insight. Her somewhat rueful conclusion is also a fairly common reaction. 'The concept of scale is far more complex than it was first envisaged. This is where the main fault of the lesson lay.' As I suggested in an earlier discussion, the analysis of teaching tasks in terms of the nature of the concepts one is trying to teach frequently raises questions that touch upon epistemological issues, and often brings to light misunderstandings about the nature of apparently well-understood concepts in various fields, not excluding those in which the students may have graduated.

The counsellor also commented on the student's and his own work:

The first point to make is that there appears to have been a significant advance for the student in this particular case, in that she seems to have acquired a much better grasp of theoretical principles than she had at the beginning of the (supervisory) relationship; (it is to be noted, however, that this seems to have taken place largely since she gave her video lesson). While it is not clear that this improvement was due to the counselling, it seems that the whole exercise (including the counselling but also including the need for self-appraisal in the form of a final report) had a very positive influence on the student's views.

The supervisor goes on to discuss ways in which he would modify his approach in future counselling sessions and the improvements that might be made to the student's course. He concludes:

> It needs to be stated emphatically in conclusion that I, as a counsellor, benefited from this exercise as much as, if not more than the student. It provided additional valuable insights into the processes of teaching and learning, which, although seen from a different angle, that of counsellor, are essentially the same and involve the same principles as those on which my own training (as counsellor of student teachers) had been focused.

This last comment echoes the point I made a little earlier when I spoke about group supervision and the value of having students observe and appraise a counsellor advising members of the group on their teaching. I suggest that it further illustrates the advantages of opening up teaching to scrutiny from as many different angles as possible.

The capstone of the total supervisory enterprise extends this opening-up process. Now the cameras are turned on the supervisor and a recording made of his or her counselling for later dissection by students. At this stage of the proceedings it is particularly difficult to remember which pedagogical Chinese box one is in. The complexity, however, is not artificial but a genuine reflection of reality. It will form the subject of a later discussion.

9

Towards the compleate supervisor

To contemplate the colloquy of student and supervisor in the eye of the camera is to contemplate one of the most complex of human encounters. Implicit in the discourse of supervisor and student teacher, and forming its conceptual core, is the problem of a pupil trying to learn something. But this is just the innermost of a set of Chinese boxes. In box number two is a student teacher trying to teach the pupil something. This student is trying to learn something with the aid of a supervisor. The supervisor is also trying to learn something: how best to help students to teach: box number three. But who teaches the supervisor? In places where this goes on it is usually presumptuous professors of education whose mentors are colleagues and other teachers and researchers and, in the best cases, the students they teach, the pupils the students teach and the supervisor's colleagues. This is box number four. As may be inferred, the outer box is particularly dependent upon bootstrap activity.

Booting the system

In the world of microcomputers there is a mysterious operation referred to as *booting the system*. Booting is necessary because a computer cannot run a programme or *operating system* until it is read from a storage device into the computer's memory, and to load it into the memory an operating system is necessary! This catch 22 dilemma is resolved by building the computer so that whenever it is switched on a small programme is automatically read in. This programme then loads the working programme and the computer is ready for action. It is my hope that the discussion in this chapter will fulfil the same function for supervision and help teacher educators over that first crucial bootstrapping operation to become capable of self-development as supervisors.

The discussion draws on the material discussed in earlier chapters and on the experience of developing a system of supervisor training over a period of a decade. One particularly intriguing aspect of this course was the co-operative working of students in initial teacher training and experienced teachers taking further inservice courses in the training institution. I suggest the same type of operation is open to most training institutions and, in fact, the working situation in which the course was developed was very similar to that in which most teacher educators are likely to find themselves; and the necessary resources were no more than those likely to be available to them.

However, there is an important feature of the approach to supervision and the supervisor training course that distinguishes it from the norm: it is explicitly predicated on a view of learning to teach as being much more than apprenticeship training. It also rejects the pessimistic view held by many teacher educators that the important aspects of successful teaching are dispositions and other personal qualities not amenable to teaching (Raths and Katz 1982). Its point of departure is one which conceives of a discipline of pedagogy as the proper study of teachers unifying their practice with a rigorous theory, based on principles drawn from the field of human learning that have demonstrated utility. It does not, however, suggest a one-way process of 'applying' the theory in practical situations. Theory and practice interact dialectically, each refining the other so that practitioners working with the theoretical principles in mind may add to our understanding of the principles as well as learning more about teaching by trying to embody them in their practice. If this seems rather high-falutin it is well to remember that, extraordinary as it may seem, very little has been done to bring together the work of theorists of human learning and teachers, so every little helps.

On course

A crucial consequence of taking a view of teacher training such
as this is that the concept of supervision is made more
extensive and more rigorous. It becomes more extensive
because it reaches out into the training course as a whole
rather than being restricted to its present focus of attention,
the period of teaching practice. It is more rigorous because
practical teaching becomes firmly rooted in theoretical studies
in pedagogy from which it draws its essential sustenance. The
fact that most theoretical studies in training institutions are
barren ground for those roots implies the need for a new kind of
husbandry, so before we consider the detail of any new form of
supervision it will probably be valuable to consider the type of
course that might sustain it.

Earlier chapters considered the nature of the pedagogical
studies likely to be appropriate to the type of teacher training
course referred to. Their exact nature and implementation is,
of course, a matter for the individual institutions. The
implementation will also depend on whether the course is one
extending over three or four years as in the case of the British
B.Ed. or of the nature of the British postgraduate certificate of
education (PGCE) which comprises about nine months tacked
on to a three-year bachelor's degree course.

Less tangible factors also exert potent influences in determining whether or not supervision along the lines I am
discussing here takes place. There are constraints in institutional structures and in the minds of people to prevent such
developments, as there is pressure for change and innovation
that seeks to encourage them. Constraints springing from
power relationships within and without institutions may be
major inhibitors, and ones over which logic and convincing
argument have little sway. Others may be in the nature of
logistical problems that impede implementation. Constraints
residing in the minds of people may include student expectations of transmission teaching that jar with an active and
applicable approach, as well as complex feelings by supervisors
about the low status of 'applied' disciplines in tertiary
institutions. The fear of the consequences of giving up the
power relationships inherent in current approaches to supervision may also be an obstacle. Despite the possible difficulties,

progress can be made towards a different kind of supervision, as has been evidenced in a few training institutions, and I refer briefly to some aspects of that work that readers may find useful.

I consider first some experiences from the one-year post-graduate certificate of education (PGCE). The derisory length of this course signals to all the low esteem of pedagogical studies. And if that is not enough, many British training institutions devote well over half of that time to installing student teachers in classrooms in the hope that they will catch the ability to teach through exposure to possible carriers of the condition. Much importance is attached to this experience by policy makers, but their utterances about it allude almost entirely to the necessary minimum *quantities* of practical teaching, virtually no attention being given to improving its *quality*. In particular, the 'block practice' extending over about a third of the school year is especially prized. It is difficult to find any justifying argument for these declarations so I suggest that readers examine their logic, if it can be found, before allowing them to inhibit explorations that may call their validity into question.

I did and found it unconvincing. Although, in the attempt to restructure the course I was interested in, it was obviously not possible to rejig the whole method of operating, for reasons already rehearsed, key steps were taken from the beginning and these in turn facilitated later developments and provided important formative feedback. Here I refer to those aspects of the course concerned centrally with learning to teach. Other courses such as conventional educational studies (historical, sociological, philosophical, psychological and curriculum) and aspects of teaching specific subjects continued as usual.

The course was structured so as to start with the emphasis on pedagogical theory, similar to that discussed in earlier chapters, with most work in the training institution, and gradually to shift the emphasis to practical work in school so that at the end of the year there would be a smooth transition into the probationary year. Practical work begins early in the course in a structured way as an essential aspect of the theoretical input. Great importance is attached to making early explicit links between the study of pedagogy and school work. This is done through video work in the first instance followed by small-scale teaching encounters.

A key aspect of the programme is to encourage students to examine their own values about teaching and education and to try to bring to the surface taken-for-granted assumptions about schools, teaching and the process they, as students, are going through in becoming teachers. A useful way of approaching this is for the students to read in the literature of the socialization of teachers. There they will encounter discussions about the processes they are themselves currently going through and will be able to see their particular experiences in the light of general processes. An allied concern is the need to equip students to make an informed analytical appraisal of school and classroom life. Here recourse is made to aspects of sociological and/or social psychological analysis. The paper by Zeichner and Teitelbaum (1982), arguing for training in ethnographic methods to enable students to make this kind of analysis, is a useful presentation of this approach. These two elements in the course, together with the pedagogical elements, take students into schools not just to observe, but also to appraise, question, evaluate and to experiment in teaching. These activities are taken as a basis for part of their assessed work and given substance in ethnographic and pedagogical studies that replace such sterile and irrelevant activities as three-hour examinations. Specific subject knowledge can feed into these studies, and it is my view that progress in supervision along the lines discussed in this book could well be made more quickly by subject tutors becoming interested in systematic pedagogy and developing their skills in that field, than by those educational tutors who insist on clutching their subjects to their breasts in order to preserve their academic purity.

In the first term, visits to school are day visits in which, for example, students are attached to a teacher to get an idea of a teacher's day and to a pupil to get an idea of a pupil's day. These visits resemble 'school attachment' as currently conducted in many training institutions; however the students' experience is much more theory-oriented and exploratory in nature than is usually the case. Some preliminary pedagogical and ethnographical work is started and it is thought important to vary the nature of the experience so that students visit different schools. The point of this is that only through variety can students build up comprehensive concepts of what teaching and school are like. *And their experience on the course may be the only chance they ever have of getting that variety.* The work on all these visits is regarded as the practical element in the course by the training institution and provides the material for discussion in its relationship to the theoretical principles under consideration.

The second term extends the school work. However, efforts are made to ensure that students do not become mere surrogates for school staff. They are *students* first and teachers second and their training is the paramount factor. Thus there is no monolithic block practice, but a build-up to two-and-a-half to three days by the end of term with a switch of schools half way through the term. During all this time the close link with theoretical discussion is maintained, the students being able to raise their own teaching experiences in the context of the consideration of general principles and the practice of their peers.

The final term tails off the school work but does not drop it. Students' experience of the practical and theoretical aspects of teaching and their contact with schools permit of flexibility in moving between school and training institution. Also, at this stage, the group meetings with supervisors can probe deeper in some of the subjects considered earlier and engage in practical work in schools if appropriate.

The problem of formal assessment is difficult but I believe that it should be phased out as soon as possible. I do not imply that there should be no quality control but that the lack of validity of current methods and their superfluous nature as I rehearsed in previous chapters should be recognized. I also consider that the detraumatization of practical teaching that would result from such a move would, paradoxically according to conventional wisdom about the need for assessment, have the effect of *improving* practice, not worsening it. This follows since it would remove the need many students feel at the moment to spend their time building up elaborate screens of impression management to satisfy their perceptions of the supervisor's idiosyncratic criteria of practical teaching competence. In the course I describe other means of assessment were introduced that were given more salience than conventional methods, and I discuss these methods later.

I mentioned earlier an account of the devising of a new

approach to teacher training of the type I have advocated, in which Evans (1983) describes the development of an honours B.Ed. course. The training institution was faced with a problem of developing a new course extending the three-year B.Ed. into a four-year honours course that was professional and of a high quality. Evans describes the detail of the course structure and should be consulted for information about it. The rationale and method of operation are similar to that for the course described earlier and the outcomes in terms of student commitment and professional development have been gratifying. Evans also found similar attitudes in co-operating schools, but resistance too from colleagues and some others who viewed the approach with suspicion and hostility 'even when, on their own admission, they have not read the related papers and arguments, nor attempted anything like this approach in their own teaching'. As part of his work with students on this course, Evans introduced elements of peer counselling on practical teaching with some intriguing outcomes which I shall discuss later.

Institutional co-operation

The conception of flexible teaching practice, embodied in the course described above, leads naturally to the integration of students' experience. Instead of there being calendared periods where they 'belong' to the school and other periods when they 'belong' to the college, attempts are made to devise a system in which they are able to move easily between the two. Practical teaching programmes should be devised to permit this movement. Student contact time should also be limited. If students are to make meaningful links between theoretical principles and their own practice they need time to reflect on these matters. A punishing timetable forces students into survival routines and drains the energy they need for careful analysis and appraisal of their experiences. If they are to carry out ethnographic studies of the school they are working in, they have to have time to record systematically and analyse the phenomena they are studying. Thus at times the emphasis is on college-based work and at times it is on school-based activities. College work could involve teaching experiences with children brought into college and school work could involve activities other than teaching. Thus the edges between college and school activities become blurred and co-operation between the two is enhanced.

There are problems inherent in this kind of school involvement. One of the salient ones is the concept of students as surrogate teachers, to be timetabled as any other teacher. Obviously schools cannot be expected to disrupt their lives to accommodate students, but dialogue needs to be engaged in to explore ways of overcoming administrative problems. Merely to ask schools to accept students on a different administrative basis from before is not enough. The dialogue with schools should include explanations and explorations about the nature of the new relationship. Schools should be invited to co-operate with training institutions in exploring the more flexible arrangements and their possible contribution to the improvement of teacher education. Training institutions can offer a *quid pro quo* for the schools' efforts by building up permanent links with co-operating schools that give them access to new thinking and developments in relevant fields. This liaison resembles a continuous INSET relationship but with an accent upon reciprocity since the schools must be the test beds of pedagogy and the ethnography of teaching, and the teachers are the ones most accessible to students in their attempts to operationalize theory.

In the course I described above, an approach of this nature to schools met with an enthusiastic response once the nature of what we were trying to do was explained. The teachers also recognized that to optimize their contribution they needed to learn more of what the training institution was trying to do, and they themselves asserted the need for staff development related to the supervision of student teachers. A further aspect of this relationship was a desire to foster permanent links with schools so as to create a network of pedagogical research and implementation in the act of co-operating in the oversight of students' school experience but extending beyond that into other areas of pedagogical concern. Here we benefited from another form of bootstrapping operation by the help we received through the co-operation of teachers who had previously taken courses in pedagogy and supervisor training in the training institution and then returned to schools.

Supervising supervisors

Although the road may have seemed circuitous at times we may now consider ways in which supervision as conceptualized in this book may be implemented. The discussion draws heavily on a specific course of supervisor training but I hope readers will find, as I do, that the procedures are readily transferable; any serious problems will probably relate to the institutional constraints referred to above. The extent to which there is flexibility in the organizational structures will determine the extent to which it is possible to implement the procedures without too much difficulty. I am, of course, conscious of the fact that all too often more depends on one's place in the institutional hierarchy than the merits of one's case. Nevertheless, I suggest that the general approach advocated here should be accessible to any tutor or supervisor who is prepared to invest the time and effort and I am sure that, if convinced of its worth, many colleagues will be so motivated.

I hope that the discussion in this book will be a helpful point of departure for readers new to this way of looking at supervision. If they are convinced I suggest they read further into the sources referred to in the text. In particular it will be necessary to get to grips with some current views on the nature of pedagogy and the way in which ideas from learning theory can be applied in teaching. I have tried to present what seems to me to be possibly fruitful ideas in my 1979 text, and references given there should also facilitate the reader's orientation. I do not think much time should be spent on conventional texts of educational psychology which often have only tenuous links with actual practice and try to be encyclopedic in their coverage. Deeper study of work in the fields of psychology of human learning would probably be the best next aspect of theory to merit attention by those wishing to take their explorations further. I suggest a good orienting device to these matters would be a reading of B. O. Smith's book on a school of pedagogy (Smith 1980). The point I should like to stress is that an understanding of theory of pedagogy is the first element in the bootstrapping operation for new supervisors.

I could be accused of inconsistency if I did not immediately qualify that statement. I make the point, in the book on pedagogy, that books have a limited potential for the building up of concepts. Thus, despite my conscientious attempts to provide exemplars in print of teaching, pedagogy or supervision, they are inevitably limited in their scope by the medium that carries their message. It is, therefore, important that, early in the supervisor's study of texts about pedagogy and supervision, the attempt should be made to build up the more complex skills I described earlier. Recall that the learning of concepts from expository material, even if the principles and not merely the words are apprehended is, in my catalogue, a type C skill. The supervisor in search of true enlightenment will need to take steps to acquire the more complex skills that I referred to as types B and A.

Readers should be aware that we are now about to encounter the complexities produced by the Chinese box nature of the study of supervision that I referred to at the beginning of the chapter. My point is that, although the last paragraph or two have referred to the need for a grasp of pedagogical theory, this need was related to the developing of a pedagogical orientation to *teaching* not supervision. Supervision also needs this pedagogical base, or how are supervisors to advise teachers? But it also needs those notions I discussed in earlier chapters derived from the particular study of dyadic teaching for the conduct of the counselling sessions. However, I do not see how supervisors can acquire the latter until they have acquired the former, so in a way what is being suggested is that supervisors have to proceed through the same kind of experience as their students if they are to become supervisors of the kind suggested. Therefore, in order to reduce the danger of ambiguity in the consideration of these matters, let us proceed through the ways in which supervisors might come to grips with the appropriate aspects of pedagogy related to *teaching* first and then consider the particular questions relating to the pedagogy of supervision.

Thus, for the moment, we will leave on one side questions relating to dyadic teaching and counselling and look at ways in which supervisors might extend their competence in pedagogy by building on their knowledge of type A pedagogic skills. In fact this step is also a move towards the developing of a key prerequisite skill to effective counselling: I refer to the appraisal of protocol material. Supervisors in training institutions will have access to copious amounts of suitable protocol material. They will see many students on practical teaching, and they will also probably be able to record teaching by students or other teachers. Their developing of type B skills will demand that they make appraisals of that teaching in the light of pedagogical principles. This is where the instrumentation discussed in earlier chapters will be of great use. However, there is an obvious problem that one's own perceptions and appraisals may be erroneous in some way or other so that a second or third opinion would be beneficial. Tutor colleagues with the same interests would be obvious candidates for such comment, but students who have made similar studies could also be helpful. In fact the first steps in the development of a new approach to student teaching and supervision could be the kind of bootstrapping operation in which the students and supervisor construct the course together. There is no need to apologize for this. Those who believe they can devise courses *de novo* to run perfectly are deluded. Another concept from computer technology is apposite here. It is taken there that first steps will inevitably be imperfect and in need of correction, so that new work is subjected to the process of *debugging*, a somewhat inelegant word for the essential and exacting operation without which the programme would not work. (See Papert 1980.) By the same token supervisors co-operating in the development of new approaches to their task, will achieve their aims not in one fell swoop but through a formative evaluation that takes for granted a never ending process of refinement of theory against practice.

After practice in appraising protocols of teaching, dedicated supervisors will want to take the next step in internalizing pedagogical principles and acquire the appropriate type A skills, that is, teaching in ways that embody those principles. Some tutors may consider that this step is not strictly necessary since their central interest is in improving their ability to supervise. I suggest, however, that they give this some thought since the main point of trying to implement the principles in this context is to enhance one's understanding of them. If two or more supervisors work together in this way their teaching can be used as each other's protocol material and, with video recording, can build up an interesting network of viewing, appraising and discussion of theory and practice of great value in enhancing individual understanding. But also, a matter of great importance, it brings teaching and supervision out of the closet, where both have languished far too long.

This spirit should carry over into the work specifically aimed at supervision. After the first step of acquiring the concepts relating to dyadic teaching and counselling, counsellors need to take steps to acquire the type B skills appropriate to counselling. The point of this is to enhance their grasp of the theory and practice of counselling. Observing others counselling either in the flesh or in video recordings is the way to tackle this and, of course, this is where co-operation with like-minded colleagues is a great help. Observing oneself counselling via the use of videotape is perhaps even better. But that observation must be directed and informed by the systematic application of principles seen as relevant to the task. This is where the schedule *Guide for Enhancing Supervision* may be helpful.

The final step is to carry out supervision oneself, employing methods incorporating those principles of pedagogy one finds congenial. This supervision should be subject to scrutiny and comment by one's peers and should, wherever possible, be video recorded to provide protocol material for self-appraisal by supervisors as well as by colleagues and students. The last remark may cause some eyebrows to rise, but surely it is a very legitimate element in a course of teacher training if we are serious in our aim to develop teaching as a high-level, theory-based, professional activity with the possibility of general application. If student teachers develop the ability to make a reasoned critique of a counselling session, then their grasp of teaching is that much more profound. Counsellors subjecting their work to this kind of appraisal will, in discussion with their students, be sharpening up their own competence as well as that of the students.

The last box

A brief account of a course that has employed methods of this type may provide a little more helpful detail. The difference between this course and what I have been describing is that it was a formal course with one person acting as course tutor to a group of experienced teachers making a study of supervision. The course tutor was also tutor to a group of students taking an initial teacher training course in the humanities. Both groups comprised people from different fields of subject studies, the unifying factor in both groups being the common field of study, teaching in the case of the students, teaching and supervising in the case of the experienced teachers. After an initial period of familiarization with principles of human learning and pedagogy, linkages were established between individuals in the two groups so that the experienced teachers liaised with one or two students on initial training. The students were learning to teach, the teachers were learning to supervise. Both went through the procedures I have described earlier in discussion of courses of initial training and of the processes of supervision and counselling.

The one feature of this course that may not figure in developments in supervision generally is the mounting of a counselling of the counsellor session. Mention has been made of this earlier. I now provide more detail.

After students and teachers have gone through the process of teaching and supervision, recordings of the supervision and the teaching are viewed by the course tutor who prepares himself to advise the trainee supervisors on their counselling, using the *GES* as a guide. He then sets up a session in which he counsels the counsellor on the counselling of the student teacher. The session takes place in the group of trainee supervisors and is recorded on videotape. During the session the course tutor observes, as well as he is able, the procedures that I have discussed earlier as being important in counselling sessions for teachers, with the complication that the session is discussing counselling and not teaching in the broader sense. After the counselling, the group discusses the counselling, usually taking the trainee counsellor's views and feelings about the interview first. The recording is available to the group to reinstate particular incidents in the same way as has been described in relation to other interviews. The recording is of greater value than just for reinstating the interview, however. The use of two cameras and split-screen techniques makes available views of the interaction otherwise impossible by presenting full-face images of the two people involved *simultaneously*. Thus a much more comprehensive picture of the interaction is provided than one person observing direct can obtain.

A measure of the complicated nature of the operation may be provided by reference to the use of protocol material in the form of short sequences of video recordings of lessons and counselling sessions. In the counselling sessions the course tutor makes use of excerpts from a recording of the counsellor counselling a student to illustrate points about the counselling and also as material for the trainee counsellor to appraise, as in the appraisal of teaching protocols. We thus have a nested series of pedagogical interactions, the course tutor drawing on material from the counsellor's counselling to advise the counsellor and the counsellor drawing on material from the student's teaching to advise the teacher. As I mentioned earlier, many of the sessions take place in groups, although the trainee supervisors and their students generally meet on their own to plan and to record the counselling sessions. The recordings of teaching, supervising and counselling of supervision are available to the groups for discussion as protocol material of varied approaches to teaching. All this work is intended to enhance the depth of understanding *of all participants* of the nature of teaching.

Many of the constraints I referred to above may preclude the widespread development of courses of supervision such as I have just described. Nevertheless I hope this will not deter those interested in attempting a bootstrap operation that approximates to that course. A co-operative and open approach will go a long way towards facilitating the self-development so vitally needed in this field.

Hardware

I may have spoken rather glibly about the use of video recordings in the development of counselling so it might be useful to devote a little attention to the subject, to indicate to readers the way in which it is used and possibly to allay anxieties that some people who are not familiar with it may have. I imagine, however, that there are many fewer in this category than when we started work in this field a decade ago and found that, even then, with much more cumbersome equipment, it was not really a problem.

The first point I wish to make is that the television recording equipment is a tool. The technicians that serve it and the students and teachers using it who fancy their chances as TV producers must be dissuaded from their fantasies. This is supremely important if the whole operation is not to be ruined. Simplicity is the key note. The idea is for any student or teacher to be able to operate the equipment satisfactorily within a day or two so that it is in fact seen as a tool and it is realized that the recording is not an end in itself but merely a very useful means to a very important end. In view of the cosmetic factor discussed by Fuller and Manning (1973) it is productive for the students to make recordings of themselves in a period of playing with the equipment so that they become familiar with the system and their own appearance on TV before the serious work starts. The set-up usually comprises two unmanned cameras, one with a wide angle lens taking in the pupils and one normal or telephoto lens focused on the teacher. A continuous recording of the teaching episode or counselling session is made without benefit of would-be producers zooming in and out to create 'dramatic' effects. The two cameras give a front view, of both the pupils and the teacher on a screen split horizontally, so that the teacher is able to see his or her own activity and the pupils' reactions at one and the same time. In the recording of the supervisory interview the screen is split vertically with the camera looking over the shoulders of the supervisor and the teacher so that each can see the exchange as it appears to the other, and third parties can see the interaction of the two full face all through the interview.

So far the only complicated aspect of the hardware is the equipment to provide split-screen displays. Another is the use of editing facilities so that the supervisor can take extracts with ease from the recording to use as protocol material. However, this is a relatively simple matter these days in view of the remarkable progress made in technology. It is now a simple matter to locate specific parts of the recording so that it is unnecessary to edit out portions of tape for easy access. When it comes to recording the supervisory session for future supervisor counselling by the course tutor, editing and patching provision is probably necessary although technical developments may well have removed this difficulty before this book appears in print. The use of slow motion or speed-up can be helpful at times. Stills and slow motion give an insight into nonverbal aspects of teaching and supervision that can be enormously revealing. Speeded-up playback can give an insight into the flow of movement during a lesson in the way Walker and Adelman used time-lapse photography (Walker and Adelman 1975). I find the addition of an electronic clock on the screen a further most useful addition that facilitates reference to specific aspects of the recording.

There is really very little else to say about hardware, except to emphasize the need for simplicity and portability. Our early bulky system operated at times off one plug in a nineteenth-century school. There is no virtue in this, merely that it illustrates that with existing equipment the potential is much greater.

In view of the worry some people have about the effect hardware may have on the teaching or the supervising I have, over the years, collected comments from students about the problem. A synoptic account of the material suggests that it does influence students in the first stages of its use. There is ample evidence of the cosmetic effect, and there is also evidence that some students and teachers are nervous on first being recorded in action. There are, of course, confounding factors in the latter effect since, in both cases, most students and supervisors were also venturing into new territory and attempting to deploy embryo skills before others so the stress was, understandably, considerable. However, there is also evidence that after experience of working like this the stress diminishes and the cameras are ignored. There seem to be few problems relating to pupil reactions to the equipment. The overall view after using recording in work such as I have been describing is one of unconcern by most people.

The last point I should like to make on this subject relates to the effects of video work. I have made the point before, but I think it is so important that it is worth reiterating. It is that the use of video feedback on its own is of limited value. Used merely to play back a student's teaching, it resembles a narcissistic form of *Sitting with Nellie* in which, instead of watching a master teacher, students watch themselves. It is not surprising that investigations into the effects of video feedback alone suggest it has little value. The Fuller and Manning survey concluded that focused feedback by supervisors was effective. However, the focused feedback in that study did not make use of pedagogical principles such as have been discussed here. Video recordings used in the way I have outlined, in conjunction with structured instruments of appraisal and underpinned by a systematic theory-based pedagogy, are a different kettle of fish altogether because they are part of a system of instruction, not its be all and end all.

Aspects of assessment

I have been rather dismissive of conventional approaches to the assessment of teaching. So far it has not been necessary to comment on the assessment of supervision since the formal evaluation of supervision does not exist in Britain. One hopes and prays that if it does become fashionable to evaluate supervision, the forces of darkness will not prevail by imposing three-hour written examinations! In a modest attempt to pre-empt such a catastrophe I should like to spend a little time on the subject here.

One problem is knowing where to draw the line. What constitutes supervision? Current thinking would probably consider it to comprise that part of a tutor's work that relates directly to the advising of student teachers in respect of their classroom teaching. I realize that this statement is also open to discussion. Should it be taken that students' understanding of the contextual aspects of teaching, such as the nature of the classroom life in which they find themselves in practice schools, be taken into account? Or the nature of school institutional structures? Or the school's social environment? These matters relate to the students' ethnographic studies discussed earlier. It seems to me that they cannot but impinge upon students' practical teaching but, except in the extreme case, their influence will not be central. On the other hand, knowledge of principles of human learning is absolutely central, so my approach to the assessment of supervision focuses on the nature of student/supervisor interaction related to the enhancement of classroom teaching, with particular reference to its relationship to relevant theoretical principles. This conception is wider and deeper than most current views, as I have suggested earlier, as is the conception of student teaching. So, in my view, should be the evaluation of both, and in fact similar approaches to their evaluation may be used.

This is consistent with the view of supervision as a form of teaching.

The approach to the assessment of student teaching and supervision that I propose is one that takes into account these conceptions. I have suggested that the assessment of teaching as currently practised by supervisors should be abandoned. This is no advocacy of the lowering of standards. The reverse. Evaluation takes as central the need for students to demonstrate in their teaching and their assessment of their teaching, a knowledge of pedagogical principles that is likely to be of abiding usefulness when they have left the training institution. The procedure I have found useful is to present students' lessons as pedagogical problems, as genuine investigations into aspects of teaching. Students are asked to take a lesson from their practical work in schools, to make a detailed study of its planning and execution and to make an analytical appraisal after teaching, using video recordings as protocols of their teaching. Their teaching is also observed by the supervisor but this is not the main element in assessment. Students write up an account of this work and the report forms a key element in their teaching and course assessment. This report comprises the following main sections and the example is taken from course material given to students.

1 A discussion of the key literature related to teaching in the chosen field.
2 A discussion of the preparatory phase of the teaching including:
   2.1 A statement of the teaching objectives.
   2.2 An analysis of the teaching task.
   2.3 An indication of the proposed procedures using any schedule thought appropriate.
   2.4 An indication of the rationale of the proposed method of assessing pupils' learning.
3 A report on the interactive phase. The actual teaching should be recorded either on audio or video. The report gives an account of the way the lesson went, drawing on the recording to compare the teaching as it happened with the plan. It also reports the results of the evaluation (did the pupils learn?).
4 Evaluation is a crucial phase. This section should

critically appraise the whole exercise in the light of theoretical ideas from the fields of pedagogy and human learning. It should be analytical not descriptive and try to identify the reasons things went as they did. It should also make suggestions for future teaching based on what was learned in the exercise.

Students carrying out work of this kind are making a rigorous study of the theory and practice of teaching in its most potent exemplification: their own. It is not only conducive to the development of students' insight, it also provides invaluable material for the supervisor to use in advising the students. Reports of this type, together with the recording of the teaching, provide a richness of material for the appraisal of teaching that is completely different from that provided by conventional student lesson notes and atheoretical discussion after the teaching. As far as formal assessment is concerned it renders obsolete the current twin-headed methods of assessment for theory and assessment for practice. Further, unlike current methods, it looks ahead. It takes assessment not as a once and for all judgement but has as a central focus the degree of insight students have into their strengths and weaknesses, as revealed by the profiles of their teaching styles provided by their peers, by their supervisors and, via the report on practice, by themselves and their understanding of methods they could adopt to improve. This understanding, I suggest, is of far greater importance than a student's rating on a subjective, and probably invalid, intuitive or printed rating scale.

The method of evaluation is also applicable with modification to supervision. This is only as it should be given the view of supervision as a form of teaching. Their guide to action resembles that of the students. The main difference is in the need to relate it to the literature of supervision and dyadic teaching. The supervisor's report thus follows the general line of that of the students but draws on the schedule *Guide for Enhancing Supervision* as well as schedules appropriate to the teaching of the students being counselled. No attempt is made to assess the interactive phase of supervision on its own. Instead the whole process of supervision is appraised as a unit and, as with the student teachers' work, the key element is taken to be the critical and analytical self-appraisal.

With both groups every effort is made to de-emphasize formal assessment and to use evaluation in its formative sense. Both types of operation are small-scale empirical investigations which enable the people concerned to learn something about teaching or supervising through their own efforts, with, of course, a little help from their friends. I suggest that this point is important because it signals to both students and supervisors that teaching is a form of investigation, not a skill to be learned once and for all and then repeated ritually until retirement. The idea of teaching as pedagogical enquiry is a powerful one that could transform teaching, and supervisors could be major agents of change in the process. The idea of teacher education in its broader sense as enquiry oriented complements this view, and offers the possibility of breaking out of the apprenticeship mode at the institutional level (Zeichner and Teitelbaum 1982).

Perhaps the products of both courses, by beginning teachers and supervisors, epitomize their nature. They are the only products of any examination system I have ever wanted to keep and I have copies of many of the reports of the empirical teaching and supervisory explorations. Not for any sentimental or patronizing reasons, but because they tell me something about teaching. It may not always be a great deal, but the important thing is that each account is a record of a unique event that can help shed light on the work of others. Ploughed back into the instructional system it can help the work of generations of students that follow, a more satisfying outcome than the descent into the shredder where most such products wind up. The recordings linked to the reports in addition provide protocol material that enriches the work of later cohorts of students. I cannot help but think that if training institutions were doing this on a larger scale we might be more effectively helped towards an understanding of teaching than by many current approaches to teacher training and research projects, including the one-off three-year funded projects looking at global aspects of teaching. I hope that some readers will feel sufficiently interested to put the question to the test by doing something similar themselves.

Evaluations

In this book I have tried to draw together information about *supervision.* In the process I imagine that I have indicated fairly clearly that I am not happy with the expression and its current connotations. I have used it because it is familiar. I have also talked about counselling and counsellors when discussing the interactive phase of supervision and feel happier with that. Probably *adviser* more accurately describes the function of the supervisor as I see it, that is, an expert who assists, with no implication of tutelage. I have also set out my own views on needed changes in the way supervision is currently conducted. Naturally I hope readers will find the substantiating argument sufficiently cogent to make their own explorations.

Experience of the work I have described encourages me to make one or two general comments that I will augment by reference to students' evaluations. Probably the crucial thing is the need for a common framework of pedagogical knowledge. I acknowledge that this probably reflects the influence of my own predispositions, but their repeated reference to the help derived from it suggests that it is of real benefit. Special mention was frequently made as to the value of clear objectives and task analysis. Protocols have also proved of immense value for student teachers and for supervisors. Supervisor behaviour and student teacher behaviour both change radically as a result of their pedagogical studies, towards systematic application of principles of human learning. More than on most courses of teacher education, the student teachers had a fairly clear idea of the degree to which their pupils learned and were more able to decide on ways of improving it. An example of this, taken from a probationer teacher's evalution of counselling along the lines I have discussed, will illustrate this last point. The teacher was in his first year of teaching and his supervisor was a teacher acting as his teacher tutor. She was also taking the course in supervision discussed above. The probationer reports:

> Possibly the most important factor to emerge from the counselling sessions was that they allowed me a great deal more confidence in my approach to teaching. This was, to me, a very valuable outcome as I feel that as a probationer my teaching possibly suffered through being rather tentative. I found that using schedules soundly based in

learning theory gave me confidence that my approach to a topic using the schedules would lead to meaningful learning taking place. I also found that I now had a precise means of analysing learning outcomes. This in turn meant that if I found any part of my lessons failing I was able to locate accurately the reason.

Many students and supervisors thought that the use of protocols was a particularly valuable part of the course. A supervisor taking the training course explained:

> The most valuable part of the course for me was the facility of viewing and discussing protocols of teaching with my peers. Their diverse backgrounds enabled an exchange of ideas to be brought to each viewing situation which served to focus attention on the way in which their ideas agreed with or differed from one's own.

I have referred in previous pages to other comments by students and supervisors on their experiences of working in the ways I have outlined. Undoubtedly the general reception is very favourable. But is this approach to supervision effective? This question is not easy to answer. The only real proof is whether or not pupils learn effectively and the evidence we have so far is that this is the case. Perhaps of greater importance, however, than current outcomes, is the point made by the probationer, that he felt able to diagnose the reasons for the failure of pupils to learn, a skill which is absolutely crucial for the improvement of teaching and which is utterly dependent upon a knowledge of pedagogical principles.

In conclusion I should like to refer in a little more detail to the modest but intriguing experiment I mentioned previously that brings together several aspects of the work on supervision I have been describing. The investigation was carried out by the supervisor who had been implementing the B.Ed. course described earlier (Evans 1983). The students had taken a course in pedagogy, had been introduced to the counselling techniques discussed here and had counselled one another on their teaching. Video recordings of counselling were shown to teachers who were not informed about the identities of the participants and they were invited to comment on them. The general reaction was that the counselling was very good but that the college had laid on its most experienced people to do the counselling. In fact, both counsellors and counsellees were students. And, of considerable importance, they were varied as to main subject of study and age of pupils for which they were training to teach. Thus a student training for infant work was counselling a subject specialist training for secondary work. The important thing was that they were focusing on the teaching and this ensured that pedagogical matters were paramount and subject and age levels less important which, as I have said before, stands some views currently fashionable on their heads.

One other point may interest readers in training institutions who may be sympathetic to the ideas about supervision expounded in this book. The supervisor just referred to was developing the approach in his college in a bootstrap operation such as I have mentioned earlier. He had had the advantage of working with others on an inservice course but the initiatives were his own. Others have done similar things. Thus it is possible for individuals to start work along these lines on their own, although it is clearly preferable if one or two colleagues are involved.

Perhaps one of the most significant outcomes of all flowing from the close study of supervision is the phenomenon referred to by the supervisor who said that the experience of studying supervision had given him a profounder insight into teaching. In the case of the student teachers' peer-supervision, it seems that there is a two-way process at work: pedagogical studies give insight into supervision and supervision gives insight into pedagogy. Both, I suggest, are crucial for advances in the quality of teaching.

References

ACEVEDO, M. A. *et al.* (1976) *A Guide for Conducting an Effective Feedback Session*, Austin, University of Texas Press.

ACHESON, K. A. and GALL, M. D. (1980) *Techniques in the Clinical Supervision of Teachers*, New York, Longman.

ALLEN, D. W. and RYAN, K. A. (1969) *Microteaching*, London/New York, Addison-Wesley.

ALLPORT, G. W., VERNON, P. E. and LINDZEY, G. (1960) *A Study of Values: A Scale for Measuring the Dominant Interest in Personality*, Boston, Houghton Mifflin.

ANDERSON, H. O. (1972) 'The supervisor as a facilitator of self-evaluation', *School Science and Mathematics*, 72, 603–16.

ARGYLE, M. (1973) *Social Interaction*, London, Methuen.

ARNOLD, R. (1981) *Teacher Training and the Primary School Curriculum*, London, Department of Education and Science, mimeo.

BAILEY, G. D. (1979) 'Maximizing the potential of the videotape recorder in teacher self assessment', *Educational Technology*, 19(9), 39–44.

BALES, R. F. (1950) *Interaction Process Analysis: A Method for the Study of Small Groups*, Cambridge, Addison-Wesley.

BEYER, L. E. and ZEICHNER, K. M. (1982) 'Teacher training and educational foundations: a plea for discontent', *Journal of Teacher Education*, 33(3), 18–23.

BLOOM, B. S. (ed.) *et al.* (1956) *A Taxonomy of Education Objectives: Handbook 1: The Cognitive Domain*, New York, Longmans Green.

BLUMBERG, A. (1974) *Supervisors and Teachers: A Private Cold War*, Berkeley, Calif., McCutchan.

―――― (1976) 'Supervision; some images of what it is and what it might be', *Theory into Practice*, November, 284–92.

―――― (1977) 'Supervision as interpersonal intervention', *Journal of Classroom Interaction*, 13(1), 23–32.

―――― and CUSICK, P. (1970) 'Supervisor-teacher interaction: an analysis of verbal behaviour', *Education* (USA), 91(2), 126–34.

BOOTHROYD, W. (1977) 'Teaching practice supervision: a research report', *British Journal of Teacher Education*, 5(3), 243–50.

BORG, W. R., KELLEY, M. L., LANGER, P. and GALL, M. (1970) *The Minicourse: A Microteaching Approach to Teacher Education*, Beverly Hills, Calif., Collier Macmillan.

BOWMAN, N. (1979) 'College supervision of student teachers: a time to reconsider', *Journal of Teacher Education*, 30(3), 29–30.

BOYAN, N. J. et al. (1973) *The Instructional Supervision Program*, Santa Barbara, University of California Press.

BRODBELT, S. (1980) 'Selecting the supervising teacher', *Contemporary Education*, 51(2), 86–8.

BROWN, G. (1975) *Microteaching*, London, Methuen.

BRUNER, J. (1966) *Toward a Theory of Instruction*, Harvard, Belknap.

CAMERON-JONES, M. (1982) Final report of primary teaching practice project, Department of Education, Moray House College of Education, Edinburgh.

CLINEFELTER, D. L. (1979) 'Educational psychology's identity crisis', *Journal of Teacher Education*, 30(4), 22–5.

COGAN, M. (1976) 'Rationale for clinical supervision', *Journal of Research and Development in Education*, 9(2), 3–19.

COHN, M. (1981) 'A new supervision model for linking theory with practice', *Journal of Teacher Education*, 32(3), 26–30.

DELAMONT, S. (1976) *Interaction in the Classroom*, London, Methuen.

Department of Education and Science (1981) *Teacher Training and the Secondary School*, London, HMSO.

―――― (1982) *The New Teacher in School, A Report by Her Majesty's Inspectors*, London, HMSO.

DIAMONTI, M. C. (1977) 'Student teacher supervision: a reappraisal', *The Educational Forum*, 4(4), 477–86.

DOYLE, W. (1979) *The Tasks of Teaching and Learning in Classrooms*, paper presented to the annual meeting of the American Educational Research Association, mimeo.

DUSSAULT, G. (1970) *Theory of Supervision in Teacher Education*, New York, Teachers College Press.

EVANS, H. (1983) 'Course extension in the B.Ed. degree: a case study', *Journal of Education for Teaching*, 9(2), 184–94.

EYE, G. (1975) 'Supervisory skills: the evolution of the art', *Journal of Educational Research*, 69 (September), 14–19.

FLANDERS, N. (1970) *Analyzing Teaching Behaviour*, Reading, Mass, Addison-Wesley.

FULLER, F. F. and MANNING, B. A. (1973) 'Self-confrontation reviewed: a conceptualization for video playback in teacher education', *Review of Educational Research*, 43(4), 469–528.

GALL, M. D. (1973) *The Problem of 'Student Achievement' in Research on Teacher Effects*, Report A73–2, San Francisco, Far West Laboratory for Educational Research and Development.

GALTON, M. (1978) *British Mirrors: A Collection of Classroom Observation Systems*, Leicester, University of Leicester Press.

GITLIN, A. and TEITELBAUM, K. (1984) 'Linking theory and practice: the use of ethnographic methodology by prospective teachers', *Journal of Education for Teaching*, 10(1), forthcoming.

GLEISMAN, D. (1972) 'The nature and use of protocol material', *Task Force 82: Focus on Educational Reform*, Washington DC, H.E.W.

GLUCKSTERN, N. B. and IVEY, A. E. (1975) *Basic Attending Skills*, Massachusetts, Microtraining Associates Inc.

GOLDHAMMER, R., ANDERSON, R. H. and KRAJEWSKI, R. J. (1980) *Clinical Supervision: Special Methods for the Supervision of Teachers*, New York, Holt, Rinehart & Winston.

GRANT, D. (1976) 'Where theory and reality meet', *British Journal of Teacher Education*, 2(3), 259–64.

GREENFIELD, W. (1977) cited in Blumberg, A. (1977).

GRIFFITHS, R. (1975) 'The training of microteaching supervisors', *British Journal of Teacher Education*, 1(2), 191–201.

HACKNEY, H. and CORMIER, L. S. (1979) *Counselling Strategies and Objectives*, Englewood Cliffs, N. J., Prentice-Hall.

HOGAN, P. (1983) 'The central place of prejudice in the supervision of student teachers', *Journal of Education for Teaching*, 9(2), 30–45.

HORE, T. (1971) 'Student evaluation: an attractive hypothesis', *British Journal of Educational Psychology*, 41(3), 327–8.

HOSTE, R. (1982) 'Sources of influence on teaching practice in the evaluation of courses in teacher education', *Journal of Education for Teaching*, 8(3), 253–61.

ISAKSON, R. L. and ELLSWORTH, R. (1979) 'Educational psychology, what do teachers value in its content?', *Journal of Teacher Education*, 30(4), 26–8.

IVEY, A. E. (1974a) 'Microcounselling and mediatherapy: state of the art', *Counsellor Education and Supervision*, March, 172–83.

——— (1974b) 'Microcounselling: teacher training as facilitation of pupil growth', *British Journal of Educational Technology*, 5(2), 16–21.

KRAJEWSKI, R. J. (1976) 'Clinical supervision to facilitate teacher self-improvement', *Journal of Research and Development in Education*, 9(2), 58–66.

LA BARRE, W. (1954) *The Human Animal*, Chicago, University of Chicago Press, quoted Bruner, J. (1966).

LANG, D. C., QUICK, A. F. and JOHNSON, J. A. (1975) *A Partnership for the Supervision of Student Teachers*, Michigan, Great Lakes Publishing Company.

LANIER, J. E. (1981) *A Futuristic View for Assessing Competence*, paper presented to the AACTE Conference: Competency assessment in teacher education, Lexington, USA, November 1980, AACTE and ERIC Clearing House on Teacher Education.

LUCIO, W. H. and MCNEIL, J. D. (1969) *Supervision: A Synthesis of Thought and Action*, New York, McGraw Hill.

MACALEESE, R. (1976) 'A note on the free wheeling effect in non-supervised microteaching students', *Research Intelligence*, 2(1), 20–2.

MCCLEOD, G. (1975) 'Self confrontation revisited', *British Journal of Teacher Education*, 2(3), 219–28.

MCCULLOCH, M. (1979) *School Experience in Initial B.Ed./ B.Ed. (Hons) Degrees Validated by the Council for National Academic Awards*, London, CNAA.

MARKS, J. R., STOOPS, E. and KING-STOOPS, J. (1979) *Handbook of Educational Supervision*, Boston, Allyn & Bacon.

MEIGHAN, R. (1977) 'Pupils' perceptions of classroom techniques', *British Journal of Teacher Education*, 3(2), 139–48.

MICKLER, W. (1972) 'New roles can facilitate change', *Education Leadership*, 29, (March), 515–17.

MILLER, J. O. (1978) *Sex Role Stereotypes*, quoted Sullivan, C. G. (1980).

MORRIS, J. R. (1978) 'The effects of the university supervisor on the performance and adjustment of student teachers', *Journal of Educational Research*, April, 67–8.

MORRISON, A. and MCINTYRE, D. (1969) *Teachers and Teaching*, Harmondsworth, Penguin.

MOSHER, R. L. and PURPEL, D. E. (1972) *Supervision: The Reluctant Profession*, Boston, Mass., Houghton Mifflin.

NORRIS, R. (1974) 'An examination of schedules of criteria related to teacher competence', *British Journal of Teacher Education*, 1(1), 87–95.

PAPERT, S. (1980) *Mindstorms: Children, Computers and Powerful Ideas*, Brighton, Harvester Press.

PARTINGTON, J. (1982) 'Teachers in school as teaching practice supervisors', *Journal of Education for Teaching*, 8(3), 263–74.

PECK, R. F. and TUCKER, J. A. (1973) 'Research on teacher education', in Travers, R. M. W. (ed.) *Second Handbook of Research on Teaching*, Chicago, Rand McNally.

PERLBERG, A. and THEODOR, E. (1975) 'Patterns and styles in the supervision of teachers', *British Journal of Education for Teaching*, 1(2), 203–11.

RATHS, J. D. and KATZ, L. G. (1982) 'The best of intentions for the education of teachers', *Journal of Education for Teaching*, 8(3), 275–83.

ROSENSHINE, B. (1971) *Teaching Behaviours and Student Achievement*, Slough, National Foundation for Educational Research.

RYAN, K. (1971) 'Supervision in a new era', *Contemporary Psychology*, (16), 556–8.

SAUNDERS, E. and SAUNDERS, C. (1980) *The Assessment of Teaching Practice: A Study*, Ulster Polytechnic, mimeo.

SERGIOVANNI, T. J. and STARRATT, R. J. (1979) *Supervision, Human Perspectives*, New York, McGraw Hill.

SHAVELSON, R. J. and STERN, P. (1981) 'Research on teachers' pedagogical thoughts, judgements, decisions and behaviour', *Review of Educational Research*, 51(4), 455–98.

SHIPMAN, M. D. (1967) 'Education and college culture', *British Journal of Sociology*, 18(4), 425–34.

SIMON, A. and BOYER, E. G. (1974) *Mirrors for Behaviour III*, Philadelphia, Research For Better Schools Inc.

SIMON, B. (1981) 'Why no pedagogy in England?', in Taylor, W. (ed.) *Education for the Eighties*, London, Batsford.

SMITH, B. O. (1969) *Teachers for the Real World*, Washington DC, American Association of Colleges for Teacher Education.

——— (1980) *Design for a School of Pedagogy*, Publication no. E–80–42000, Washington DC, US Department of Education.

SMYTH, J. (1984) 'Teachers as collaborative learners in clinical supervision: a state of the art review', *Journal of Education for Teaching*, 10(1), forthcoming.

SORENSON, G. (1967) 'What is learned in practice teaching?', *Journal of Teacher Education*, 18(2), 173–8.

STONES, E. (1968) *Learning and Teaching: A Programmed Introduction*, London, Wiley.

——— (1975a) 'Black light on exams', *British Journal of Teacher Education*, 1(3), 209–303.

——— (1975b) 'How long is a piece of string?', in *How Long is a Piece of String?*, London, Society for Research into Higher Education.

——— (1976) 'Teaching teaching skills', *British Journal of Teacher Education*, 2(1), 59–78.

——— (1977) 'Meta-metateaching, a suitable case for study?', *British Journal of Teacher Education*, 3(2), 97–109.

——— (1978a) 'Psychopedagogy: theory and practice in teaching', *British Educational Research Journal*, 4(2), 1–19.

——— (1978b) *Self Confrontation in Supervisor Training*, paper presented to the conference for the improvement of university teaching, Aachen, Germany, mimeo.

——— (1979) *Psychology of Education: A Pedagogical*

Approach, London, Methuen (previously published as *Psychopedagogy*).

—— (1981) *Educational Psychology and Teaching: A Perspective*, Washington DC, ERIC Clearing House on Teacher Education, ED198076.

—— (1983) 'Perspectives in pedagogy', *Journal of Education for Teaching*, 9(1), 68–76.

—— and ANDERSON, D. (1972) *Educational Objectives and the Teaching of Educational Psychology*, London, Methuen.

—— and MORRIS, S. (1972a) 'The assessment of practical teaching', *Educational Research*, 14(2), 110–19.

—— (1972b) *Teaching Practice: Problems and Perspectives*, London, Methuen.

—— and WEBSTER, H. (1983) *Failure and Retrieval in Teaching Practice*, mimeo.

SULLIVAN, C. G. (1980) *Clinical Supervision: A State of the Art of Review*, Virginia, USA, Association for Supervision and Curriculum Development.

TABACHNIK, B. R. *et al.* (1982) *The Impact of the Student Teaching Experience on the Development of Teacher Perspectives*, paper presented at annual meeting of American Educational Research Association, University of Wisconsin-Madison, mimeo.

THORLACIUS, J. (1980) *Changes in Supervisory Behaviour Resulting from Training in Clinical Supervision*, paper presented at the Meeting of the American Educational Research Association, Alberta, University of Lethbridge, mimeo.

TURNER, H. M. (1976) 'The implementation and critical documentation of a model of clinical supervision: a case study', quoted Sullivan, C. G. (1980).

TURNEY, C. (ed.) (1977) *Innovation in Teacher Education*, Sydney, Sydney University Press.

TURNEY, C. *et al.* (1982a) *The Practicum in Teacher Education*, Sydney, Sydney University Press.

—— (1982b) *Supervisor Development Programmes*, Sydney, Sydney University Press.

WALKER, R. and ADELMAN, C. (1975) *Classroom Observation*, London, Methuen.

WHITFIELD, T. D. (1977) *Interpersonal Communication*, Houston, University of Houston Press.

WISEMAN, S. and START, K. B. (1965) 'A follow-up of teachers five years after completing their training', *British Journal of Educational Psychology*, 35(3), 342–61.

WRAGG, E. C. (1982) *A Review of Research in Teacher Education*, Slough, NFER-Nelson.

YATES, J. W. (1981) 'Student teaching in England: a recent survey', *Journal of Teacher Education*, 32(5), 44–6.

—— (1982) 'Student teaching: results of a recent survey, *Educational Research*, 24(3), 212–15.

YORKE, E. M. (1977) 'Television in the education of teachers: a case study', *British Journal of Educational Technology*, 8(2), 131–41.

ZEICHNER, K. M. and TABACHNICK, B. R. (1981) 'Are the effects of university teacher education washed out by school experience?', *Journal of Teacher Education*, 30(3), 7–11.

—— (1982) 'The belief systems of university supervisors in an elementary student teaching program', *Journal of Education for Teaching*, 8(1), 34–54.

ZEICHNER, K. M. and TEITELBAUM, K. (1982) 'Personalized and inquiry-oriented teacher education: an analysis of two approaches to the development of curriculum for field based experiences', *Journal of Education for Teaching*, 8(2), 95–117.

ZIMPHER, N. L., DEVOSS, G. C. and NOTT, D. L. (1980) 'A closer look at university student teacher supervision', *Journal of Teacher Education*, 31(4), 11–15.

Index